CONDITIONS THAT CREATE INFLUENCE FOR PURCHASING IN CORPORATE STRATEGIC PLANNING

by
Larry R. Smeltzer
Arizona State University

ACKNOWLEDGMENTS

The Center for Advanced Purchasing Studies (CAPS) and the author would like to thank those companies that contributed to this research by participating in the case study interviews. Special thanks go to the companies that agreed to be interviewed and provided the basis for the case studies included here. This research would not have been possible without their strong support and cooperation.

Several industry supply management executives helped formulate the research or reviewed the manuscript and provided many helpful suggestions for improving its analysis and presentation. While those who contributed are too numerous to mention here, special thanks go to:

Ed Coyle, IBM Corporation
Robert Dunn, Walker Interactive Systems
Barbara B. Lang, Fannie Mae
Fred McClintock, AlliedSignal, Inc.
Helmut F. Porkert, Ph.D., Bayer Corporation

Finally, we would like to thank Jackie Wilcock, Senior Office Automation Specialist at Arizona State University and Kerri Christiansen at CAPS, for preparation of the manuscript; Carol L. Ketchum, Assistant Director at CAPS, for thoroughly editing the manuscript; and Phillip L. Carter, D.B.A., Harold E. Fearon Chair of Purchasing and current Director of CAPS, for his strong encouragement and support.

Of course, complete responsibility for the final study rests with the author of this report.

ISBN 0-945968-28-0

TABLE OF CONTENTS

FIGURES AND APPENDICES

EXECUTIVE SUMMARY •

What conditions create influence for the purchasing function in corporate strategic planning? This question was addressed for the Center for Advanced Purchasing Studies (CAPS). After 21 in-depth case studies of 24 organizations, discussions with numerous purchasing executives, a literature review, and discussions with academic researchers, CAPS researchers developed an initial model to address the question. Researchers made appropriate revisions to the initial model after the model was reviewed by nine purchasing managers and several academics. The revised model is presented in Figure 1.

Each of the boxes represent a condition or factor that affects purchasing's influence in corporate strategic planning. The diagram is presented in somewhat of a linear fashion; however, each condition affects and interacts with every other condition.

The central condition is *proactive purchasing management.* Proactive management includes those purchasing processes that add value to the overall business enterprise, seek to add quality to the products and services offered by the firm, and manage costs. These processes are implemented with initiatives such as total cost management, early purchasing involvement in business processes and new products, early supplier involvement in product or service development, outsourcing, and general involvement in business activities. Proactive purchasing adds value through the use of data management to integrate the entire supply chain. Proactive purchasing is a continuous effort to search for, develop, and take advantage of opportunities to add value to the overall business enterprise.

Proactive purchasing is the central condition that creates purchasing influence in corporate strategic planning; however, six conditions are concurrently necessary for proactive initiatives to prevail. These conditions are not separate in that each condition interacts with the other conditions.

The first two conditions are highly interactive: *competitive environment* and *executive leadership.* Competitive environment is the extent to which competing companies develop new strategic advantages or new competitors enter the market. The research indicates that when competitive forces increase, the firm attempts to find new ways to respond and further develop its own competitive advantage. One strategy for increasing competitiveness is to generate more value from the purchasing function.

Executive leadership is highly interactive with the competitive environment because top executives must believe that purchasing has the potential to increase the organization's competitive advantage. At the minimum, top executive management must support purchasing's initiatives. Ideally, top executives create an environment in which opportunities are presented and purchasing can take advantage of them. For instance, a CEO might suggest that a division's purchasing director taken on the role as a corporate lead buyer for a commodity. The director must take advantage of the opportunity.

Purchasing leadership takes advantage of the opportunities created by the competitive environment and executive leadership to formulate and implement the proactive purchasing initiatives. These two earlier conditions unlock the door of opportunity, but purchasing leadership must fully open the door to create influence within the company. Purchasing leadership includes the strategic vision and implementation tactics for how purchasing can best add value to the business. Without appropriate purchasing leadership, top executive vision is not translated into proactive purchasing initiatives.

All six of the conditions presented in the model must exist for proactive purchasing management to be implemented; therefore, it is not possible to say that one condition is necessarily more important than the others. However, strong executive leadership and purchasing leadership can create the other conditions whereas the reciprocal is not true. Accordingly, it may be said that strong *executive leadership* reacts to the *competitive environment* and creates opportunities for creative *purchasing leadership* to develop proactive purchasing initiatives. But for these initiatives to successfully add value to the organization and develop purchasing influence, the three other conditions are necessary: *competent employees, purchasing strategies,* and *tactics* that are congruent with organizational processes and culture and the correct organizational and purchasing structure.

Competent employees have a comprehensive understanding of the purchasing process. In addition, these employees have a thorough knowledge of the business and know how they may add value, can conduct thorough analysis of products and processes, can build coalitions, and know how to develop and use metrics.

Purchasing strategies and tactics must be *congruent with organizational strategy and culture.* If the organization fosters an entrepreneurial, risk-taking culture with minimal controls, purchasing must do likewise. However, if the organization supports hierarchical control with numerous policies, purchasing must be congruent with the balance of the organization. Similarly, purchasing must present initiatives and performance measures consistent with those of the organization. In a bank, purchasing must communicate in terms understood by bankers. In a high-technology manufacturing company, purchasing should communicate in terms understood by engineers.

Finally, it is necessary that the *organizational and purchasing structure* provide the proper support for proactive purchasing initiatives. To have successful proactive purchasing initiatives, the chief purchasing officer must be viewed as comparable to the top executives of the other functional areas. The CPO must be visible throughout the organization and have access to the CEO's office. Successful initiatives will lead to a higher position for purchasing within the hierarchy that, in turn, will likely lead to more successful initiatives. Within purchasing, a structure that has simultaneous loose-tight properties obtains most influence. Centralized control over some processes and procedures should be obtained; however, in other situations a decentralized structure that fosters entrepreneurial creativity is best.

When all of the conditions represented by a box in Figure 1 are simultaneously present, purchasing will have a high level of influence in the corporate strategic planning process.

MANAGERIAL RECOMMENDATIONS

As a result of this research, the following recommendations are presented for purchasing management to gain additional influence in corporate strategic planning.

1. Purchasing management should be aware of the firm's *competitive posture* to understand how purchasing may *add value* to the firm.

2. Implement *proactive purchasing strategies* that will add value to the firm. These initiatives include such activities as total cost management, early purchasing involvement in organizational activities, early supplier involvement in new products and process, long-term supplier alliances, outsourcing, and involvement in activities other than traditional purchasing. Proactive purchasing involves forward-looking activities that involve risk but add value to the organization.

   • Activities that simply procure materials and services by responding to internal customers' requisitions should be computerized if at all possible.

   • Purchasing management should always be asking itself how the purchasing function can better add value to the firm and increase its competitive posture.

3. In their leadership positions, purchasing managers should

   • possess and exhibit a high level of commitment and belief that purchasing can make a contribution to the organization;

   • become missionaries to the rest of the organization; preaching for the importance of purchasing in the company;

   • communicate to top executives in terms of executives' visions and tactics rather than in purchasing terms;

   • possess a learning orientation that consists of new ways to do business;

   • introduce and fully embrace change that will increase the value of purchasing within the organization.

4. *Purchasing strategy* must be consistent with the corporate strategy. Purchasing management should take every available opportunity to demonstrate how purchasing strategy supports and helps to implement corporate strategy.

5. Review *purchasing culture* to assure that it is consistent with the corporate culture. This may be accomplished by analyzing the accepted ways of doing business including all communications that demonstrate norms, values, and beliefs.

6. Hire and train *competent purchasing employees* who are articulate, analytical and assertive. These employees must possess knowledge of the business and its products, have good coalition-building and team skills, and be able to develop and use metrics that measure purchasing performance.

7. Design and implement a *purchasing structure* that is a loose-tight fit. This requires that purchasing be centralized for processes in which control and consistency are important but decentralized where a high level of interactions with customers is preferred.

8. Strive to possess high *visibility* throughout the organization and have easy *access* to the chief executive office. These two attributes are more important than the formal position of the chief purchasing officer within the organizational structure.

9. Because it is difficult to sell your own CEO on the importance of purchasing, support professional associations that may be better able to sell CEOs on the importance of purchasing.

FIGURE 1

CONDITIONS THAT CREATE INFLUENCE FOR PURCHASING IN CORPORATE STRATEGIC PLANNING

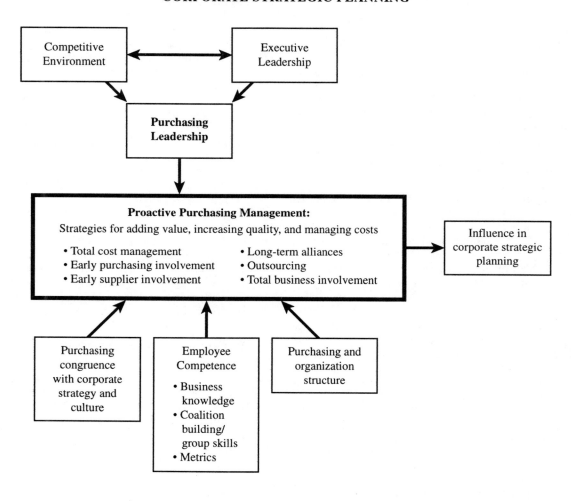

INTRODUCTION •

The purchasing function has received extensive attention in popular business magazines during the past several years. For instance, in 1995 an article appeared in *Fortune* titled, "Purchasing's New Muscle." This article makes dramatic statements about purchasing and its power to reduce costs and add value. The article quotes one executive as saying "Nothing we do is more important."[1] An article in *Harvard Business Review* presented an exposé on how changes in supplier relationships at Chrysler resulted in slashed inventories, reduced defects, and greatly improved the efficiency of its production lines.[2] Many other recent articles on the importance of purchasing could be cited.[3]

At the same time, a large number of new books are now on the market explaining how purchasing is crucial to the firm's success. For example, one book contends that by understanding the supply process, it is possible for management to implement a new way of doing business.[4] Another recent book presents numerous cases in which purchasing made a significant impact on a business and accordingly increased its influence.[5]

More attention will likely focus on purchasing as electronic commerce develops. The story of how giant retail firms such as Wal-Mart increased profit margins through electronic buying is well documented; however, this may be only the tip of the iceberg. It appears that the buying function will receive increased attention as electronic commerce becomes fully developed.[6]

The importance of purchasing has been verified with empirical research. For instance, a study by McKinsey & Company reported that the strategic management of purchasing may trim total procurement spending between 5 percent and 15 percent over a three-year period.[7] Another study states purchased materials account for an average of approximately 55 percent of total production costs in manufacturing.[8] Combine these two findings and the importance of purchasing is clearly evident. Still another study reported that almost half the companies surveyed had expanded the role of purchasing in the corporate strategic planning process.[9] After an extensive review of the purchasing literature, two authors state, "...purchasing does have an important role in corporate strategy."[10]

But a dilemma exists. The purchasing function is receiving increased attention, and numerous situations can be cited in which it has made significant contributions; however, purchasing does not appear to have high levels of influence in many organizations. Research conducted by the Center for Advanced Purchasing Studies (CAPS) indicated that many top level managers believe that purchasing is important, but the function is not seen as a major contributor in most business decisions.[11] In another study, a survey of 210 organizations found that although the purchasing function can influence at least 18 key decision issues in the organization, in only six of these issues did a majority of the purchasing functions report having total responsibility.[12] In general, it may be said that the importance of the purchasing function in corporate performance has been recognized by many different individuals.[13] Unfortunately, most nonpurchasing personnel have a very simplistic view of the purchasing function, and they understandably demonstrate little regard for internal purchasing performance measures, which they view as mainly tactical.[14]

Why is it that while purchasing seems to be getting more attention and its importance can be demonstrated, it still lacks influence in so many organizations? This recurring question was asked by purchasing executives over the past several years at the Center for Advanced Purchasing Studies Executive Purchasing Roundtable.

While executives informally discussed this question, several related terms kept recurring. The terms *influence, power, status, credibility,* and *respect* were used interchangeably. It was important to differentiate among these terms to assure that the most important question to purchasing managers was being asked. An analysis of these five terms clarified that *influence* was the best term of the five for this research.

A DEFINITION OF INFLUENCE

Why is *influence* the best operational definition for this study? Why not use the term *status, power, credibility,* or *respect?* Definitions and explanations of these terms explain why the term *influence* was used.

First, the focus of this study was on the purchasing process in total rather than an individual. In the management literature, *power* generally focuses on the individual and emphasizes control. Drawing on the common meaning of the term, *power* may be defined as the ability of a person to exercise control over another person.[15] This study was more interested in the organizational level of analysis than in the individual level, and *control* was not an issue.

Status is the social rank of a person in a group. It is the condition of the amount of recognition, honor, and acceptance given to a person. High-status people within a group usually have more power and influence than those with low status.[16]

Given these definitions of *power* and *status,* it may be said that status is a precondition for influence.

Credibility is a quality of being believable. It implies that what an individual or institution proclaims has merit. Information provided by some with credibility has validity as determined by authorities. But credibility does not necessarily suggest action. For instance, a medical doctor may be a dietary specialist. But the information she provides may not result in action.

Influence is the direct antecedent to behavior at an individual or group level.[17] Influence can be thought of as the ability to affect the perceptions, attitudes, or behaviors of others.[18] Behavior is the most important concept. For purposes of this study, influence is the demonstrated use of power toward organizational objectives.

CONTEXT

Next, the context in which influence was to be applied had to be determined. Of course purchasing influence could be exerted at various levels from the buyer to the chief purchasing officer. This study, however, was interested in company-wide influence of the purchasing function. It was not necessarily interested in the influence of one purchasing professional. Corporate strategy is the overall plan for the company to interact with the competitive environment to achieve organizational goals.[19] It also may be said that corporate strategy helps a firm to allocate its resources in order to capitalize on its relative strengths and mitigate its weaknesses.[20] Therefore, if purchasing is to have corporate- or company-wide influence, purchasing should have influence in the corporate strategic planning process. In order for planning to have influence in corporate strategic planning, it would be necessary for the function to have power, credibility, and status within the organization. When referring to organization levels of influence, corporate strategy must be considered.

RESEARCH QUESTION

Based on the interests of the Center for Advanced Purchasing Studies and an analysis of the operational terms, three important concepts emerged: *influence, corporate strategic planning,* and *purchasing.* As a result, this research question was addressed:

What conditions create influence for purchasing in corporate strategic planning?

BRIEF LITERATURE REVIEW

Only a brief literature review is presented here for two reasons. First, the purpose of a literature review is to present the previous literature relating to the research question and indicate how the study will enhance the existing research. Little research has been done that directly relates to this research question. Much of the literature that relates to the final model will be presented when the model is discussed. Second, the literature review should present a theoretical framework for the research. Too frequently, one hears the comment that "this research is useless because it is too theoretical." On the contrary, good theoretical research helps direct the investigator in the search of understanding.[21] Theory is inherently practical and applied because it highlights the important concepts and relationships found in a problem situation.

A theoretical framework that directed the design of this research is described in the research methodology section. The theory that relates to the final model is briefly presented when the model is discussed.

Most of the related literature either suggests that purchasing should be more strategic or it provides approaches for it to become more strategic.[22] It does not investigate how purchasing influences corporate strategy. Only one article specifically looks at the sources of purchasing managers' influence within the organization.[23] This article first presents a theoretical discussion of power and influence, and then it reviews industry and firm characteristics that affect influence. This article presented five practical guidelines for purchasing managers:

1. Understand the key forces in industry structure, especially in terms of bargaining power of suppliers and intensity of rivalry.

2. Understand the firm's strategy.

3. Understand the departmental structure and the department's informal role.

4. Understand the backgrounds of top management people.

5. Understand your own strengths and weaknesses.

Although no formal hypotheses were established for this study, this particular article influenced the type of information that was sought in the initial case studies.

DESIGN OF THE STUDY •

RESEARCH PROCEDURES

After the research questions were developed, a research methodology had to be designed that would best answer the question. To paraphrase a renowned researcher, a good research question implies that a researcher will be working with an uncertain, shifting, confusing, and exasperating phenomenon.[24] Because it can be a confusing phenomenon, neither speculation and conjecture nor simply a systematic investigation is sufficient. A valid research design is necessary. In selecting and implementing a research design, it is imperative that researchers not use a particular design simply because it is an approach with which they are comfortable. Rather, the researcher must ask, How can I best obtain information that will help managers address their problems?

A variety of research designs may be used as it is generally accepted that various versions of seven different designs exist.[25] The researcher should design the methodology based on the nature of the research question or hypothesis, the level of proof required, the time permitted to conduct the study, the size of budget allocated, the number and skill of support personnel available and so on.[26]

Users of research knowledge should not be forced to evaluate the design; rather, they must trust that the researcher has developed and implemented the appropriate research design. The user of research knowledge should be able to ask and answer positively, "Do I have confidence that this information will help me with the *who, what,* and *where* of a question?" The insights provided by the information also should help the user answer the all-important *"why"* question.[27]

Qualitative Versus Quantitative Designs

One of the first questions addressed when developing a research design is whether a quantitative or qualitative design will best answer the question. In business research we often think of survey questionnaires when considering quantitative designs. The primary advantages of a survey questionnaire are (1) data may be obtained from a large sample of the universe, and (2) the quantitative data obtained make statistical comparisons possible. However, four conditions must exist for a survey to be successful: (1) the research question must be highly structured, (2) the researcher must know the correct questions to ask, (3) the number of questions asked must

be limited, and (4) the number of surveys returned must comprise a representative sample.

Conversely, qualitative designs usually involve in-depth investigations of an unstructured nature using a limited sample (seldom exceeding 20 sample points). The analysis makes no attempt to be representative of the entire population; rather, the investigations are frequently meant to be impressionistic rather than definitely analytical. The goal is to understand the texture and nature of the phenomenon in a holistic sense, rather than to numerically measure and analyze a predetermined set of variables. The nature of qualitative research makes it ideal (1) in exploratory stages of the research, (2) when many complex, interrelated variables may be involved, (3) when in-depth probing is required, and (4) when socially sensitive topics are investigated.

Case Study Methodology Selected

The most appropriate procedure for this research question is the case study method. In this situation, the case study method allowed in-depth analysis of the phenomenon involved within a select number of organizations. Specifically, the interview case study method was chosen to gather data because it is an empirical inquiry that can be used to (1) investigate a contemporary phenomenon within real-life context, (2) investigate the boundaries between phenomenon and context, (3) employ multiple sources of evidence and (4) conduct in-depth probing of the sources.[28]

Qualitative Methodology

The study was conducted using generally accepted qualitative techniques.[29] Information was first obtained from key individuals in the organizations using a semi-structured interview. During the first interview, a list of other key individuals was developed, and important written information such as organizational charts, mission statements, product portfolios, and business plans were obtained.

As a first step, three pilot case studies determined the general strategy for obtaining cooperation from the host organizations and the type of information desired. However, with qualitative procedures, the type of information obtained evolves as the study proceeds. It is important that the researcher maintain an open mind throughout the case studies so that bias does not develop toward the criticality of information. The frequency with which words, phrases, and trends were mentioned and their relative emphasis was noted.[30]

Much is said about employees' perceptions and their interpretations of events in the organization by the examples and stories they present. Especially important is the manner in which employees refer to other groups and functions within the organization. Accordingly, special attention was given to employees' stories and metaphors.

One disadvantage of this study design is that it did not allow the researchers to conduct a longitudinal study. Valuable information would have been obtained if interviews and documents could have been collected prior to and after significant organizational events. However, time and monetary limitations precluded this research design.

The case studies continued until saturation of information developed. However, saturation was difficult to achieve in this study because of the complexity of the issues addressed. New information was obtained from each of the first 16 cases. After these first cases, several organizations within the same industry were analyzed as one case. This procedure was followed for two cases and then three single company cases were conducted. At that point, saturation was reached.

In qualitative research, validity and reliability are more difficult to precisely measure than with quantitative research. Qualitative assessment is largely the product of the interaction between the judge and the phenomenon. Both validity and reliability lie in the judges' qualifications.[31] In this study, the primary judge possessed extensive experience with qualitative research. The researcher had conducted several funded research projects, published a number of articles based on this methodology, and made academic presentations on this research methodology.

Research Sample

The goal with the case study method is to obtain cooperative participants who will allow access to extensive, relevant information. Attempts are made to gain a representative sample; however, the time and cost of each case study precludes the possibility of obtaining a highly representative sample. A trade-off is made between in-depth information from each source within a smaller sample compared to a larger sample from which less information is obtained.

For this study, opportunistic sampling was used to gain access to cooperative organizations.[32] Several criteria guided the selection of participants. First, the company had to exceed $250 million in annual revenues. It was believed that a smaller company might be inordinately influenced by one factor. In the final sample, the smallest company had more than $500 million in annual revenues. Second, the company could not have been acquired within the past four years, nor could it have merged with a similar sized entity. Third, the company had to be willing to allow researchers access to employees at various levels of the organization. Fourth, the purchasing executives had to be willing to provide names of individuals who might not be "friends" of the purchasing function. Fifth, the initial employees contacted and all subsequent contacts within the companies were told that all information would remain confidential. Only general information that would preclude identifying the company would be disclosed. However, the company had to be willing to disclose any information the researcher considered pertinent to the study.

In case study research, it is essential to obtain information from an array of companies and make inferences from data gathered at these points. As an initial step in the sample selection, it was necessary to identify those organizations in which the purchasing function could be considered most influential in the corporate strategic planning process. To identify these companies, an inquiry about the more advanced organizations was sent to the Center for Advanced Purchasing Studies (CAPS) 1995 North American Executive Purchasing Roundtable participants. Because of the financial commitment required to attend the Roundtable, the assumption was that the more progressive U.S. companies would attend the Roundtable. In turn, it was assumed that these individuals would be familiar with the purchasing functions that would be most involved in the corporate strategic planning.

The arbitrary criterion was that if more than two respondents identified a company, this could be considered a progressive organization. Sixty-six letters were sent to Roundtable participants and 22 responses were received. In these 22 responses, 14 companies were identified more than twice. In addition, the participants in a small-group discussion at an annual North American Roundtable were asked to identify companies that were most involved in corporate strategic planning. Organizations were identified as highly progressive organizations from these two sources. Seven of these organizations were included in the case.

Other sources were drawn on the basis of industrial representation. The ideal was to have a broad representation from major industries. The industries represented in this study are presented in Appendix A.

Development of Dependent Variable

In quantitative research, the dependent and independent variables are identified and measurement procedures established *a priori*. In qualitative research, the dependent variable hopefully can be developed *a priori*, but the variable may evolve as information is gathered. In this study, efforts were made to develop the dependent variable *a priori* by discussing the research with academics conducting research on purchasing management and interviewing supply management executives.

The key terms in this study were *influence* and *strategic planning,* which are difficult concepts to objectively evaluate. Accordingly, a number of proxies were used that could contribute toward assessment of the concepts. Following is the list of items used to assess *influence* in the context of *strategic planning* for this study.

1. The vice-president of purchasing, or CPO, reported directly to the chief executive officer.

2. The chief purchasing officer was a member of the most influential planning or executive committee in the organization.

3. The chief purchasing officer was at a level in the organizational structure that was at least comparable to other functional departments such as marketing and human resources.

4. The company was willing to invest in the function by hiring a chief purchasing officer who had comparable experience and educational background as other functional directors. (This criterion was used as a substitute for salary because actual salary would be too difficult to determine.)

5. The chief purchasing officer and other purchasing employees were involved in a number of important decision-making committees throughout the company.

6. A qualified purchasing group was defined by the employee's level of experience, qualifications, and emphasis on professional development.

These proxy measurements were used to assess purchasing's influence on a scale of one to 10. The assessments and the reasons behind them are presented for each case in Appendix B.

REVISION OF THE INITIAL MODEL

When 21 in-depth case studies of 24 organizations had been completed, an initial model was developed in an attempt to explain the conditions that create influence for purchasing in corporate strategic planning. This model and explanation is presented in Appendix B. After the initial model was developed, it was decided to follow two additional steps. First, all of the case notes and related information were reviewed once again to determine how they fit the model. While reviewing the case information, extensive follow-up information was obtained from select case organizations through telephone interviews.

After the initial case notes and follow-up information were acquired, the model was reviewed with chief purchasing officers and their managers from four highly respected purchasing operations. These organizations were drawn from the list of progressive purchasing organizations derived from the Roundtable participants. Managers with a variety of career backgrounds and from diverse organizations were represented in these discussions. In total, nine managers with more than 200 years of experience in 11 organizations were involved in these discussions.

The purpose of the review was to evaluate the model by gaining in-depth feedback from experienced executives who had high levels of influence in their organizations. To minimize potential bias, general overview questions were used. But specific follow-up questions were used where conflicting information existed. A brief summary of these discussions is presented in Appendix C.

After the follow-up discussions and additional case inquiries were conducted, a revised model was developed. This model is presented as Figure 3.

CONDITIONS THAT CREATE INFLUENCE FOR PURCHASING IN CORPORATE STRATEGIC PLANNING •

RESULTS AND DISCUSSION

The 21 in-depth case studies of 24 organizations, follow-up interviews, and reviews with additional purchasing managers resulted in the model presented as Figure 1. A brief explanation of this model is presented in the Executive Summary. The purpose of the following discussion is to more fully explain and discuss each of the conditions. In addition to discussing the conditions, the placement of the conditions in the model is explained.

An important point about any model is that it is only a representation of reality. Because this is an initial study of the conditions that create influence for purchasing in corporate strategic planning, this model must be considered an educated approximation of reality.

This model is presented in a systematic, linear fashion and allows for only partial identification of organizational phenomena. Organizations are complex webs of written policies, procedures, and human interactions that are, at best, difficult to map. In reality, the phenomena presented in this model interact with one another in many complex ways. However, this model is presented in a systematic, linear manner to help us understand a complex phenomenon and partially remove the sense of chaos about the research question.

The first condition discussed, and the one most central to this model, is proactive purchasing management.

PROACTIVE PURCHASING MANAGEMENT

The concept of *proactive purchasing management* initially was difficult to label. Such concepts as opportunity, adding value, risk, initiative, and strategy appeared in the case studies; however, it was difficult to put a collective label on the concepts. It gradually became clear that these concepts were attached to a set of purchasing actions or strategies including total cost management, early purchasing involvement, early supplier involvement, long-term alliances, outsourcing and total business involvement.

Proactive was the title put on these collective concepts. The following discussion reviews what is generally meant by the term *proactive* and why these purchasing initiatives were termed proactive. A comprehensive discussion of this concept is presented later because it is central to the entire model.

Purchasing managers are encouraged to be proactive in this era of quickly changing corporate environments. Nearly 20 years ago the claim was made that purchasing managers needed to develop a more proactive strategic approach.[33] As recently as 1993, sentiment had not changed, as researchers encouraged a proactive approach to purchasing planning.[34] But what is proactive purchasing management?

Examination of purchasing textbooks gives us part of the answer. Leenders and Fearon,[35] in their purchasing text, discuss five major categories of purchasing substrategies: assurance-of-supply, cost-reduction, supply-support, environmental-change, and competitive-edge strategies. They also discuss many specific strategic purchasing opportunities that could be considered proactive. Examples include backward vertical integration, outsourcing, establishing supplier quality assurance programs, supplier development, supplier-purchaser data sharing, and risk-sharing with the supplier. Heinritz, Farrell, Giunipero, and Kolchin,[36] in their purchasing text, identify several substantial risks that occur when purchasing is not included in the strategic-planning process. These risks include threats to supply assurance, possibility of improper supplier selection, problems with environmental constraints, increased company liability and uncertainty of supply and lead time. When we combine these strategic outlooks, a view of proactive purchasing begins to emerge. The concepts that emerged in the case studies seem to be associated with a strategic perspective.

In a recent textbook, Dobler and Burt provide additional insight about the term *proactive*.[37] They contend that the purchasing discipline is moving from a purchasing transaction to a supply management perspective. In this process, two transitions in focus are occurring:

(1) a shift in focus from internal processes to value-adding benefits, and

(2) a shift from tactics to strategy.

Again, this fits with the cases. *Value added* was a term used frequently in those cases in which purchasing had high levels of influence—concepts labeled as *proactive management were present.*

The 1984 book *Proactive Procurement* by Burt[38] highlights the importance of proactive purchasing management. Burt focuses on the importance of developing integrated systems for design, procurement, quality, inventory management, and production in order to move from a reactive purchasing activity to a proactive profit-making procurement system, and to add value to the firm's operations. Burt seems to use the term *proactive* synonymously with *integrated systems*. He states:

"The procurement of material and services is a process that cuts across organizational boundaries....

"Integration of the activities performed by these departments results in a synergism....

"Implementation of an integrated procurement system results in proactive procurement, as distinguished from reactive purchasing."[39]

In 1996, Burt teamed with Pinkerton to co-author a book titled *Strategic Proactive Procurement.*[40]

Here they define proactive procurement management as the process of professionally and aggressively adding value during the four stages required for effective procurement: (1) the determination of what to buy; (2) the identification and development of the appropriate relationship with the desired source of supply; (3) obtaining the lowest total cost associated with purchasing and converting the required material or service; and (4) ensuring that the required material or service is received in the required time and that relations with preferred suppliers are developed to ensure these suppliers' availability for future procurement.[41]

Again, this is directly related to what was found in the case studies. Specifically, those companies that were included early in various processes, such as new product development, were more influential and considered proactive. Also, where purchasing was involved in many different business processes it was more influential in corporate planning. As an example, in one case purchasing was even involved in the development of a new corporate logo.

The concept of proactive purchasing management is directly addressed in a dissertation by Carr.[42] She defines proactive purchasing as purchasing's willingness to take risks and its ability to effectively use current knowledge to make decisions about the future.

After reviewing extensive literature, she concludes that purchasing proaction includes purchasing foresight and purchasing's willingness to initiate change. In Carr's study of purchasing strategy, one hypothesis is that purchasing proaction is positively related to the level of strategic purchasing present in the firm. She asked purchasing managers to indicate the strength of their agreement with the following statements which represent the proactive purchasing factor:

1. Purchasing is eager to take risks when appropriate opportunities are present.

2. Purchasing professionals pursue company objectives relentlessly even though it may not win favor from fellow managers in other functions.

3. Suppliers are involved in the design process of our product.[43]

The results indicate that the managers who agreed with these statements also managed more strategic processes. In some ways, what is termed strategic is also proactive.

The characteristics identified by Carr as proactive were identified in the cases where purchasing had more influence. In Case M, for example, purchasing was extensively involved in outsourcing of nontraditional items. This was a high-risk endeavor for two reasons: (1) a large dollar value was involved where a high possibility of failure existed, (2) other departments could resist the initiative.

Case K is an example where the purchasing director relentlessly pursued corporate goals at the risk of offending the human resources director. Purchasing became involved in contracting temporary employees as a strategy for reducing expenses. In the cases where purchasing was involved early in new product design, purchasing generally had more influence in strategic planning (Cases P and U).

Another possible way to understand proactive purchasing management is to look at its opposite: reactive management. So let us first examine reactive purchasing management. One author states that purchasing is too frequently reactive to the needs of others in the firm, but he does not provide an operational definition of the term *reactive.*[44] Others state that when the purchasing department is viewed as providing a buying service within the firm, the function is reactive.[45]

These two comments assist us with the meaning of reactive purchasing management, and a general theme begins to emerge from various authors. One way to view reactive purchasing management is to think of the purchasing function as only reacting to internal customers. This is the traditional approach in which the purchasing department receives a purchase order from some other department within the firm and proceeds to place that order with a supplier. The purchasing group then follows the purchasing process to ensure that the order is placed and the goods are received in a timely manner.

If goods are not received on time, a crisis may develop, during which purchasing reacts to the scenario created. In this situation, the purchasing department is largely a transaction-oriented, clerical function that services other functions and assumes little risk. More time is spent expediting than planning. Purchasing reacts to the requests of internal customers, and, as a result, the clerical purchasing function has low status in the firm.[46]

The reactive purchasing function is largely evaluated on two criteria: administrative expenses and savings on material expenditures. Because of the importance of administrative costs, typical metrics are *requisitions filled per employee, cost per requisition,* or *total number of employees per dollar spent.* Material costs and deliveries are important, so the general measurement is cost reductions accomplished by the purchasing group. Accordingly, negotiation skills that result in lowered costs are important to the reactive department. This was the situation in Cases E and F and influence was low in both cases.

So what is the opposite of the reactive purchasing? *Proactive management* may imply that purchasing does not wait for top management to make requests to the purchasing group to reduce costs; rather, purchasing acts before receiving directives. Case J is an example where purchasing acted before receiving directives.

The general conclusion is that proactive purchasing management includes those initiatives that involve risk and look toward the future. Rather than simply billing purchase orders, proactive purchasing is involved in decisions on what to buy. Proactive purchasing management integrates total cost management and strategies for reducing total cost.

Proactive purchasing is central to the model on conditions that affect purchasing's influence. The remaining conditions reviewed here each affect proactive purchasing.

COMPETITIVE ENVIRONMENT

An initial hypothesis was that differences between industries would largely explain the different amounts of influence that purchasing has in corporate strategic planning. It seems obvious that purchasing and materials management are more important in some industries than in others. Or stated another way, purchasing would have more influence in corporate strategic planning in those industries in which materials are a major component of the strategic plan.

When first designing this study, the researchers asked many different purchasing managers why purchasing would have more influence in one company than another. Although no formal notes or records were kept, an obvious trend emerged in the manager's responses, which was consistent with the research literature.[47] Materials are simply more important in some industries than others. In other words, if the ratio of goods purchased to total expenses was high, purchasing/materials management would be more important than if the ratio was low. Accordingly, firms in which purchased materials are a high portion of total revenues, we would expect purchasing to have more influence in corporate strategic planning.

In addition to informal conversations with purchasing managers and the limited research, Porter's five force model of competition adds further insights about company differences.[48] At the center of his model is price competition. On either side of price competition are buyers and suppliers (see Figure 2). A particular firm within an industry can experience price competition at any time. A natural reaction when experiencing price pressure is to reduce price more quickly than the competition.

Assume that a firm is experiencing increased competition. If the firm's purchasing function can reduce material price, it will have more influence within the firm. But it is not always possible to immediately reduce material prices. The bargaining power of suppliers might be so great that purchasing has little power to reduce price. This could occur if one or more of the following conditions occurs:

- Suppliers are dominated by a few large companies and are more concentrated than the industry to which they sell.

- Satisfactory substitute products are not available to buyers.

- Buyers are not a significant customer for the supplier group.

- Suppliers' goods are critical to buyer's marketplace success.

- The effectiveness of supplier products has created high switching costs for buyers.

- Suppliers are a threat to integrate forward into the buyer's market...suppliers may develop products that compete with the buyer.

If any of these conditions exists and price pressure exists in the industry, we would expect that purchasing would not gain additional organizational influence because there would be little that purchasing could do to reduce material prices and assist the organization to become more competitive.

FIGURE 2

FIVE FORCE MODEL

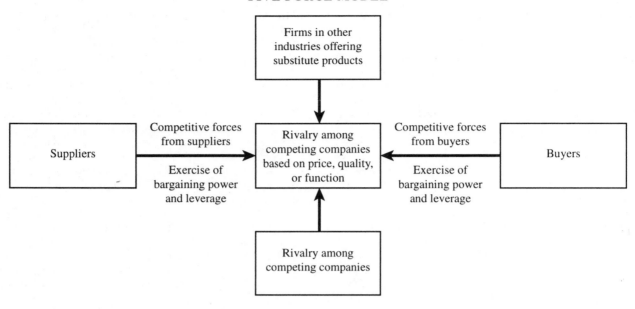

Source: Adapted from Michael E. Porter, "How Competitive Forces Shape Strategy,"
Harvard Business Review 57, no. 2 (March-April 1979) pp. 137-145.

However, if the following conditions exist, we would expect buyers to have bargaining power. In turn, purchasing would enhance its organizational influence because it would hypothetically be able to assist the organization to reduce prices or increase quality.

A buyer organization is powerful when:

• It purchases a large portion of an industry's total output.

• It could switch to another supplier's product at little or no cost.

• The suppliers' products are undifferentiated or standardized, and the buyer poses a credible threat to integrate backward into the supplier's industry.

These informal conversations and the limited literature led to the following formal hypotheses:

Hypothesis 1. Purchasing is more influential in those organizations in which the ratio of materials purchased to total cost of goods sold is high than in those organizations in which the ratio is low.

Hypothesis 2. Purchasing is more influential in those organizations that have greater power over suppliers.

This case study research did not confirm either of these hypotheses. For instance, in a financial/information firm (Case M), purchasing had high influence while in a high technology manufacturer organization (Case E),

purchasing had extremely low influence. This is not what would be expected. However, this is not to say that industrial dynamics were not important. The dominating theme seemed to be price *competition* within the industry. This is somewhat consistent with Porter's Five Force model. Purchasing became more influential when the industrial competitors were reducing price or increasing quality, a potential new entrant emerged, or substitute products were developed.

Case T provides a prime example of a firm in which new entrants into the market created a competitive force. In turn, the company had to either reduce price or increase quality. Purchasing gained attention as it was seen as the function that could enhance the company's competitive posture.

In several case studies, mere survival was an issue (Cases U and D). A radical strategy had to be implemented just to survive, so cost reduction was an obvious alternative. In these cases, purchasing/materials management is going to obtain influence.

Several cases demonstrate that when price and/or quality pressure developed within the industry, top management had to find quick solutions and turned to purchasing. Cost and quality alternatives were analyzed that heretofore had been unexplored. Because of the existing inefficiencies, it was possible to reduce costs by improving purchasing processes. Purchasing gained influence because it made an observable contribution.

Case K is a prime example where a firm did not have a high ratio of purchases to revenue, but the influence of purchasing began to emerge. With Case E, little competition existed in the industry for either quality or price, and purchasing had little influence. In Case A, price and quality competition were severe and purchasing was rather influential.

Still another reason may explain why purchasing may have influence in an industry where materials is not a large portion of expenses. This may be termed *industry tradition.* The hospitality industry discussed in Case Q provides an example. Traditionally, materials/purchasing had not received much attention in one firm while in another it had always had a highly visible role. What could explain the difference? Both firms operated in the same industry, and little difference occurred at either firm when the top level executives retired. The difference may be a matter of long standing tradition.

In summary, the initial hypothesis relating to industrial dynamics was not supported. Rather, competition is an important aspect of purchasing's influence in the organization. The contributing dynamic is the competitive pressure within the industry and not the nature of the industry itself. Porter's model of industrial competitiveness helped explain competitiveness in relationship to the research question.

In Figure 1 of the Executive Summary, a two-directional arrow was drawn between *Competitive Environment* and *Executive Leadership.* This arrow represents the influence that the two concepts have on each other or the *interaction* of the two concepts. A competitive environment may influence an executive's perception of purchasing. Retroactively, executives may influence the way that the competitive environment affects the purchasing process. For example, in Case M, the company was facing price competition. A new executive believed that the only way to remain competitive was to reduce expenses. The CEO perceived purchasing to be an important function in reducing costs. The CEO and the competitive environment interacted to increase purchasing's influence.

The two concepts—competitive environment and executive leadership—may act independently to affect purchasing's influence. However, in these case analyses, the two concepts generally interacted. The impact of executive leadership was greatest when the organization was facing inordinate competitive pressures. The impact of the competitive environment was greatest when a dynamic leader developed a strong executive initiative to meet the competition. We now review executive leadership in more detail.

EXECUTIVE LEADERSHIP

The impact of top executive leadership was a major theme in a majority of these cases. A new executive had a significant effect in seven of the cases, and in other cases the top leadership provided strong support for purchasing. For instance, in Cases N and O the CEO had long supported the purchasing process and in Case U the CEO increased the influence of purchasing by hiring a new chief purchasing officer. In each of these cases, purchasing had high levels of influence in strategic planning.

Conversely, low levels of influence on strategic planning were related to low levels of support from the CEOs' offices. This may be seen in Cases E, G, Q, and R.

During one of the interviews, a vice-president of purchasing stated, "A vice-president can pound on the door forever, but he won't get in until the CEO opens it." This quote summarizes the influence of the CEO. It was not necessary for the CEO to establish the initiatives or even present the opportunity for them; however, it was necessary for the CEO to open the door to the proactive purchasing initiatives. For instance, in Case B the CEO seemed to generally ignore the purchasing initiatives even though effective and efficient practices were being introduced. Overt support would have enabled the CPO to increase leveraged buying in a more efficient manner across the smaller business units. This may be compared to the situation in which the CEO attended several purchasing council meetings. His presence demonstrated support.

The literature addressing purchasing influence hypothesized that executive leadership would be important in the answer to the research question.[49] Little doubt exists about the *importance* of the top-level executives. However, different opinions exist about the *role* of top executives. Is it more important for top executives to have and communicate a vision or to establish and communicate specific results and expectations?

In his book, *The Fifth Discipline,* Peter Senge points out the importance of a vision when he says that a vision creates a sense of "...what we are and what we want to create." He goes on to say that as a result of a vision, work becomes a part of pursuing a larger purpose embodied in the organization's products and services.[50] A research study found that visionary firms, as a group, performed 55 times better than the overall stock market, and taken individually, performed eight times better than their non-visionary competitors.[51]

Despite this observed link between vision-driven action and performance, some high-profile executives reject the notion that a corporate vision is important. Shortly after taking over as CEO of IBM, Louis Gerstner, Jr., stated, "There's been a lot of speculation as to when I'm going to deliver a vision of IBM. The last thing IBM needs right now is vision."[52] Gerstner believed that what IBM needed most was a return to basic "blocking and tackling" skills, such as reducing costs. Chrysler's CEO, Robert Eaton, has voiced agreement: "Internally, we don't use the word *vision*. I believe in quantifiable short-term results—things we can relate to—as opposed to some esoteric thing no one can quantify.[53]

Whether the person in the CEO's office is a visionary or more interested in short-term results, it is important that the purchasing profession communicate to CEOs in terms of both visions and results. Purchasing managers generally are not accustomed to communicating in terms of vision. To quote one operational vice-president who was interviewed during a case study, "Don't tell me how much you have saved me...tell be what you have done to help me build a better company." What was this person looking for? Probably something that could tell him how purchasing would support both the company's vision and short-term goals.

The ultimate question becomes, "How can the potential impact of the purchasing function best be communicated to the CEO's office in order to increase purchasing's influence on strategic planning? This must be done differently for different types of CEOs — visionaries are interested in one type of information, while those most interested in tactics are probably interested in operational procedures.

Will it be necessary for executives with purchasing experience to be in the CEO's office before the function can open the door and obtain influence? Logically it would be easier to communicate with those who had experience in purchasing. But this could become a circular argument...more purchasing executives will not be assigned to the CEO's office until the function is more influential. Furthermore, in this study no relationship was noted between the CEOs' purchasing experience and purchasing's influence in strategic planning.

So how can the purchasing profession communicate to CEOs the importance of purchasing? Remember the comment cited earlier that it is difficult for an internal manager to open the executive's door? Will it be necessary for professional organizations to communicate to top executives on behalf of the managers? Will CEOs pay more attention to an article in *The Wall Street Journal* or *Harvard Business Review* than to memoranda from their own managers? This research was not designed to find a way to open the executive door so that purchasing could obtain additional influence. However, it is essential that the purchasing profession address this question if it is to gain additional influence.

PURCHASING LEADERSHIP

Purchasing Leadership was a major theme in nine of the cases in which purchasing was highly influential in corporate strategic planning. It is the condition that leads to or allows for proactive management as a result of the competitive environment and executive leadership. Accordingly, it is a mediating variable between competitive environment, executive leadership, and proactive management. Purchasing leadership is printed in bold capital letters because it is a key linking condition in the model. Regardless of the competitive environment and executive leadership, purchasing would have little influence if it were not for purchasing leadership.

Proactive purchasing management and purchasing influence increases dramatically when competitive environment, executive leadership, and purchasing leadership are integrated concurrently. Or stated another way, the power of each condition multiplies with the other conditions to generate a synergy for proactive purchasing management initiatives.

Case P is an example where a competitive environment, a supportive CEO, and strong leadership resulted in a highly influential purchasing function. In this case, it cannot be said that one condition led to the other. In fact, it may be the "chicken or egg phenomenon" in that it cannot be determined which occurred first. As mentioned earlier, however, the purchasing leader is probably limited in the extent of influence that can be obtained without a supportive executive.

Case O is an example where strong leadership resulted in only moderate influence. In this situation, the competitive environment was not intense and the CPO received limited support. Because of the purchasing leadership, however, purchasing rapidly gained influence during the leader's tenure with the company.

What attributes identify a purchasing leader that can leverage the other conditions to obtain purchasing influence? Hundreds of articles and books have been written on leadership. Attributes of a purchasing leader probably do not differ significantly from leaders in other functions.

Based on these cases, numerous discussions with executives, the purchasing literature, and the leadership literature, three attributes of effective purchasing leaders are presented: (1) institutional commitment, (2) a learning orientation, and (3) an understanding of the business. In an organization with *institutional commitment*, the leaders had almost a missionary zeal for purchasing to make a value-added contribution to the company. They wanted to make a difference. This is consistent with the findings of a recent review of the research literature on leadership.[54] This review identified traits of successful leaders, and one of these was a high level of personal drive to contribute to the organization.

A learning orientation is the second characteristic listed for successful leaders. Change was a major theme in each of these cases. Some managers accepted change, others embraced it but still others created change. Within this last group, the leaders have a vision for purchasing within the organization, are excited about the possibilities, and institute changes so they can realize their visions. This is comparable to what is generally referred to as the learning orientation. The learning leader provides for almost constant resource mobilization to handle a barrage of change. But they don't need to overhaul the entire system to implement the change.[55]

As the title *learning* implies, the learning leader is striving to learn about new ways of doing business. The learning leader is not afraid of the change that is required to implement the new practices. In the various cases, the leaders for whom the title *learning* would apply were members of various organizations in which they could learn and share new ideas. They were often well-educated but looked for new ways to educate themselves.

Through this learning paradigm, these leaders seemed to have a vision for purchasing. These case studies revealed leaders who did not want to be bound by conventional wisdom. Some quotes heard from managers at organizations where purchasing had high levels of influence follow: "We want to develop a progressive, value-adding supplier management strategy. We don't know what it is, but that won't stop us." Another manager said, "We want this company to be identified for its supply management practices," and "I want business schools to study cases on the creative way we work with suppliers." These quotes help identify what is meant by a learning orientation to leadership.

The third characteristic is an understanding of the business. The leader must have a thorough knowledge of the processes and products of the business in order to increase the value added by purchasing. The leaders in influential purchasing groups all had extensive experience either in their present industry or a related industry. This is consistent with the leadership research literature that states knowledge of the company, industry, and technology are important leadership traits.[56]

In 12 of the 21 cases, the chief purchasing officer had joined the company relatively recently. These 12 companies received an average rating of approximately 8.3 on the one-to-ten rating scale for purchasing influence. The conclusion could be that either highly effective leaders had been hired by the company or that the leaders joined already highly influential purchasing groups. A review of the cases indicates that the first conclusion is more accurate. When new CPOs joined the company, they implemented immediate changes. This group represented the leadership traits cited: dedication to making a contribution to the organization, a learning orientation, and a knowledge of the business.

Generally speaking, the CPOs in this group did not necessarily have an extensive background in purchasing. In

fact, several of the 12 were relatively new to purchasing. However, they generally had related experiences within the industry and had a learning orientation. Information from this study indicates that it is not necessary for the chief purchasing officer to have an extensive purchasing background for the function to have a high level of influence.

In summary, we first discussed *proactive purchasing management* as a condition that affects the extent to which purchasing has influence in the strategic planning process. Proactive purchasing includes risk and looks toward the future. It includes such initiatives as total cost management, early supplier involvement, and long-term alliances. It is central to the influence model, so all of the other conditions are preliminary to proactive management.

Two of the preliminary conditions are *competitive environment* and *executive leadership*. Competitive environment is the extent to which the firm is experiencing competitive pressures. If executive leadership believes that purchasing can help the firm improve its competitive position, it will support purchasing's initiatives and increase its influence. Each of these two conditions interact to affect *purchasing leadership*. The characteristics of purchasing leadership that lead to greater influence are industrial commitment, a learning orientation, and understanding of the business.

The next three conditions to be discussed are *purchasing's congruence with corporate strategy, employee competence,* and *organizational and purchasing structure.*

PURCHASING'S CONGRUENCE WITH CORPORATE STRATEGY AND CULTURE

"We have to be on the same page as the rest of the business." This comment is similar to others such as, "When we talk to the marketing people, we have to be marketers or when we meet with the engineers, we have to be engineers." Another comment heard during the case studies was, "We have to know what is in the top executives' heads. What are their priorities?" These and many similar comments were saying that it is important for the purchasing function to be synchronized with the rest of the company.

Two aspects of purchasing must be linked with the company for purchasing to obtain and maintain influence in corporate strategic planning: corporate strategy and organizational culture.

Corporate Strategy

In seven of the company cases, a changing strategy was directly related to the level of purchasing influence. In Case J, purchasing was synchronized with the strategy, and purchasing had high influence. Meanwhile, in Case F, it appeared that the corporation was pursuing a different strategy than the overall corporation.

The importance of a congruent strategy is not limited to instances where the strategy is changing. In one situation where the purchasing group had high influence, the senior purchasing managers spent six months analyzing the entire corporate strategy to assure the purchasing strategy was in alignment with corporate strategy. When asked how they assured that the strategies were aligned, the managers explained numerous corporate and purchasing plans and displayed documents to show the congruence. In Case S, the CPO asked the chief operating officer to review the purchasing strategy. The key here is that the CPO initiated the review. In general, where purchasing influence was high, the CPO placed a great deal of emphasis on the relationship between the purchasing and corporate strategy.

In addition to observing the relationship between purchasing and corporate strategy in the cases, the purchasing research literature emphasizes the importance of this link. After reviewing the connection between corporate and purchasing strategy, several authors state that it is imperative that purchasing's operational plans and policies support the corporate strategies.[57] Others have developed a conceptual framework that demonstrates the importance of this process.[58] In addition, a research-based model assumes that the most sophisticated purchasing strategy is one that is integrated with the corporate strategy.[59]

The case studies reported here and the research literature conclude that purchasing's influence will increase when the purchasing strategy is isomorphic with the corporate strategy. Unfortunately, often the interrelationship does not exist. A recent study found that the supply management policy often exists independent of the firm's corporate strategy.[60] The conclusion is that this is probably why purchasing often lacks influence in corporate strategic planning.

Organizational Culture

Culture is the set of values, guiding beliefs, understandings, and ways of thinking shared by members of an organization.[61] Culture exists at two levels. On the surface are the visible behaviors and documents such as written objectives, mission statements, and action plans. But these visible elements reflect employees' deeper beliefs, assumptions, and thought processes. Both these external and internal levels integrate employees throughout the company. However, if the culture is not consistent throughout the organization, members of the organization will not work well together.[62]

Different cultures are appropriate for different organizations; however, it is important that the chosen culture is agreed upon by all elements of the organization.

In the cases analyzed for this study, when purchasing had a high level of influence in corporate strategic planning, purchasing had a strong culture that was consistent with the organizational culture. And the converse was also true, when purchasing influence was low, little emphasis was placed on culture. Cases P and G are two diverse examples of organizational culture. During the interviews at Case P, the same quotes were heard a number of times, "If they can, we can too." *They* referred to the competitor, and this phrase was seen on various internal documents. The competitive nature permeated the company. Several references were made to the company being number one in its industry and the purchasing group being world class. Stories were told about the executives that reflected the assertive, competitive nature of the company. Also, a review of various documents indicated a strong connection between the values of the purchasing group and the overall organization.

In Case G, meanwhile, little mention was made about the organization as most conversations referred to purchasing. When one manager was asked to reflect on the overall value of the organization, he simply said that he wanted to do well. Another individual in the purchasing group believed that the company had no overall beliefs or values. But documents could be found in other parts of the organization indicating a theme that could be identified as an *adaptability culture*.[63] By this it is meant that the company focuses on the external environment through flexibility and change to meet customer needs. This emphasis was not seen in the purchasing culture.

Another example is provided by the healthcare cases. Three hospitals were analyzed for this case. The purchasing group in each hospital had low influence in the strategic planning process. But the conclusion could be made that the *mission* culture was not consistent between the hospital in general and the purchasing group. The mission culture places major importance on the shared vision or purpose. The purpose of a hospital, in general, is to provide healthcare services. The mission of the purchasing group was to provide cost efficient and effective delivery of materials and capital equipment. A difference existed between the two missions.

In any organization, purchasing has a culture and hopefully a strategy. To obtain and maintain influence within the organization, purchasing must have a strategy and culture that is consistent with the company as a whole.

EMPLOYEE COMPETENCE

In nearly every case, employee competence was a theme. In some cases, the employees were able to implement a proactive strategy and obtain influence because they possessed the requisite skills. In other cases, opportunities were not realized because the employees did not possess the necessary skills. For instance, in Case A, the company was experiencing major strategic changes, but the employees did not have the correct orientation to take advantage of the situation. In Case D, many of the better employees left the company as a result of a reorganization.

Meanwhile, in other cases, major emphasis was placed on developing employees so that they could implement new initiatives. In Case U, for instance, employees were sponsored to participate in graduate education while in Case L employees were encouraged to earn their C.P.M. In Case H, all the employees were required to invest time in additional training. Meanwhile, in other cases, extensive emphasis was placed on hiring highly qualified external employees. This was the situation in Cases P and N. In particular, with Case N, the new employees put pressures on the existing employees to increase their skill sets.

The importance of competent employees for obtaining influence is clear in these cases. But the type of skills required is also important. When discussing the importance of competent employees with Case U, it was stated, "We need the three A's: analytical, articulate, and aggressive." This is a nice summary of the evidence that emerged from the cases. This set of skills or aptitudes is probably not much different from most other business functions. And the importance of employee competence in purchasing is well documented in many different ways. For instance a study sponsored by the Center for Advanced Purchasing Studies (CAPS) found that employee training programs assisted companies in developing purchasing initiatives.[64] The extension of that CAPS study is this study on purchasing influence because purchasing initiatives are related to purchasing influence. In other words, it may be said that highly trained employees lead to purchasing initiatives which in turn leads to purchasing influence.

Three other aspects of competent employees emerged: understanding of the product and business, the ability to work in groups and develop coalitions, and the ability to develop metrics.

Business Knowledge

In Case E, purchasing had a low level of influence, and it could be said that purchasing employees did not understand the product. To quote one employee when discussing a piece of capital equipment, "We order them, we don't need to really understand them." This statement was at the other end of the continuum from Case M where the first thing new employees did was spend extensive time learning the product and business. Also, in Cases Q and R, emphasis was placed on the importance of understanding the industry. It could be concluded that a thorough understanding of the product and the business was a clear difference between a proactive and a reactive purchasing group. Case I also emphasized the importance of product knowledge. This is consistent with a research project which found that technical product knowledge is central to an employee's success.[65]

Another concept that emerged was an understanding of the business. At first, it was difficult to determine what this meant. Gradually, however, it was concluded that some people understood how value may be added to the business process while others don't understand the overall process. This does not mean that people understand debits and credits; rather, it means that good employees understand how purchasing fits into the overall process and what it can do to help the company meet its corporate mission.

Coalition Building

Three related themes were detected during the case analysis: horizontal influence, coalition building, and teams. In each instance, reference was made to employees' ability to generally influence others throughout the organization. For instance, in Case B the CPO made continual reference to the ability to sell ideas. In Case K it was indicated that purchasing considered it extremely important to get on the proper teams throughout the company. In Case C, purchasing believed that it lost influence because of the team emphasis, and in Case D no doubt exists that purchasing lost much influence as a result of teams. Influence was gained in Cases H and J.

Coalition building and teams were important at each organizational level. As mentioned earlier, in Case B the CPO talked about the importance of his team's involvement. Meanwhile, in Case P involvement was just as important to the entry-level employee as it was to the most senior purchasing employee.

Findings from these case studies are consistent with other research in purchasing. For instance, a survey of 210 companies found that a transition from an individual to a team approach was taking place in many different purchasing functions.[66] In a study that looked at future trends, again the conclusion was that teams and coalition would become more important for purchasing as the "functional silos" become obsolete.[67] In general, extensive support is available that supports the power of cross-functional teams.[68] However, this previous research had not indicated that the teams would increase purchasing's influence.

Metrics

Employees had to know how to measure their impact on the organization and communicate it to the correct people. Case K and Case O are two examples of this. In Case K, several new sophisticated employees had joined the company, and one of their first charges was to develop proxy measures that indicated purchasing's impact in the organization. The CPO believed that it was important to always be looking for ways to develop new measures. In Case O, the belief was that to be important or show an impact, any initiative had to be measured. This firm recently hired several young purchasing employees that were extremely strong in measurement techniques. This was also the situation in Cases U, M, and H.

The important point is that a high level of employee sophistication is required to develop appropriate metrics. More sophisticated measures than the ratio of dollars spent per employee are required.

The importance of metrics has also been supported by research findings. The authors of a research project on future purchasing trends state that metrics will become increasingly important and sophisticated.[69] Research has verified that it will be important to know how to both develop and use measurement to influence internal customers.[70] No doubt exists that purchasing employees must be able to develop and use metrics correctly in order to have influence within the organization.

PURCHASING AND ORGANIZATION STRUCTURE

Structure in this context refers to design of the organization. It is the relationship among people, tasks and functions. Or stated another way, how are the departments arranged within the company, what are their tasks, and where are the centers of responsibility and accountability? In today's organization, a formal and informal structure generally exists; however, in this discussion we are primarily interested in the formal structure.

Centralization refers to a structure in which authority and decision making are focused around one individual or a small group. When authority and the power to make decisions is distributed to many individuals at different levels within the organization, the structure is said to be decentralized.

No right structure exists for all organizations. Most authorities on organization structure would say, however, that effective organizations are characterized by three design attributes: *simple form and lean staff, decentralization to increase entrepreneurship,* and *simultaneous loose-tight properties.*[71] *Simple form and staff* means that the underlying form and systems of effective organizations are elegantly simple, and few personnel are in staff

positions. *Decentralization* encourages innovation and change as creativity and innovation in employees at all levels are encouraged and rewarded. *Simultaneous loose-tight properties* may seem like a paradox, but effective organizations use tight controls in some places and loose controls in others. For instance, a purchasing group may have specific ethical standards and spending authorizations. Yet, in other areas, employees may be free to experiment, to be flexible, and to take risks in ways that can help the company reach its goals.

First we will discuss structure within the purchasing organization and then the placement of purchasing within the overall organization.

Purchasing Structure

Evidence from this case study research supports the idea that loose-tight organizational properties are appropriate for purchasing organizations and will lead to the most influence. In 16 of the 21 cases, centralization/decentralization was a major theme. But this is not to say that either a centralized or a decentralized organization structure led to more or less influence. Rather, a combination of structures is best for influence.

Recall that a central component of proactive purchasing management is risk taking. In order to foster risk taking, a decentralized or loose structure is appropriate. However, with decentralization, power is distributed throughout the organization. Power is a prerequisite to influence. So it would appear that a dilemma exists: Should purchasing decentralize and lose influence or centralize and lose creativity and risk-taking orientation which is essential for proactive management? Neither. It can do both and achieve a loose-tight fit. It can centralize in some areas and decentralize in others. Or to quote one manager interviewed for this study, "We are a centralized purchasing group, but we appear decentralized to most of the organization."

Case S provides an excellent example of a loose-tight fit. The purchasing strategy and guiding procedures were developed by a centralized team. But purchasing employees were on many teams throughout the company and physically housed away from the central purchasing office. This gave them access to their customers. At times they worked with their customers so closely it appeared they were part of their customer's group. This allowed them to appear decentralized. In addition, purchasing implemented a credit card system and computerized MRO purchases to the extent possible. This allowed them to decentralize the acquisition of materials throughout the organization, but it remained under the control of purchasing.

Case I is another example of a loose-tight fit. With this company the purchasing function was again centralized. To the extent possible, procurement activities were centralized through advanced information technology such as a credit card system. But the purchasing employees were extensively involved with make-versus-buy decisions as well as new product teams. To be successful with these activities, it was best for some purchasing employees to be housed close to marketing while others were housed near production. The purchasing group appeared to be decentralized. However, they remained committed to the purchasing process as they worked closely with small teams throughout the company. An important point is that in both of these companies, purchasing had a high level of influence in corporate strategic planning.

In Case D, many purchasing employees believed that they lost influence when purchasing was decentralized. Unfortunately, when the function was decentralized, little centralization was maintained. Accordingly, low levels of power and influence were retained by the purchasing function. It would have been better to attempt a loose-tight fit rather than *either* decentralization or centralization.

As organizations stress teams and empowerment that result in flatter organizations, it will be important for purchasing to retain centralized control of strategy, policy development and certain procedures. In particular, it will be essential to gain centralized control through advanced information technology. Concurrently, the proactive purchasing group will keep informed of decentralized purchasing activities through information technology.[72]

If the company does not have a loose-tight fit, more influence is gained through a centralized function than a decentralized function. Cases J and M provide evidence for this. However, it should be emphasized that most evidence points toward a loose-tight organization resulting in the best condition for proactive purchasing management that leads to influence in corporate strategic planning.

Organization Structure

When discussing organization structure we are interested in the position of the purchasing function in relation to the top executive positions and other comparable functions. For many of us, organization structure implies functional groupings. In this traditional arrangement, functional structures are grouped together by common function from top to bottom. All engineers are located in the engineering department, all of marketing in another department, production in another department, and so on. This traditional perspective is generally considered the essence of a bureaucracy.

The functional structure promoted economies of scale; however, innovation is slow because of poor coordination, and each employee has a restricted view of overall goals. The traditional functional structure began to lose favor in the 1980s because of its disadvantages.[73] As a result, the organization structure of the mid to late 1990s takes on many different forms with such titles as the horizontal, network, matrix, and hierarchy organization.

Because of the diversity of organizational structures, it was difficult to identify the center of control and authority during the case studies. As a result, the focus was the organizational position of the chief purchasing officer. But even this was difficult. For instance, Case O was a decentralized company consisting of many different business units. It could be said that each business unit had a CPO, but a purchasing director was also housed in the corporate staff. He and his staff served as the internal subcounsel and support for the various business units. He had no formal authority within the business units. But as an individual, he had a great deal of influence.

A similar situation existed in Case N. Although a person had the title of executive vice president of supply management, the position had little direct authority but much influence. In each of these situations, a combination of the dynamic leadership and access to the CEO's office lead to influence.

The critical condition within the organization structure was that the CPO seemed to be visible and accessible. This position must have visibility throughout the organization — from the CEO's office to the front-line employees. Returning to Case N, the purchasing function had high influence and the executive vice president of supply management had a highly visible position. Before taking the supply management position, he was already in a highly visible position. Subsequently, as the executive vice president, he was seen attending meetings with the CEO and generally made the purchasing process highly visible. But in each of the low-influence cases, the CPO position and the person holding the position had low visibility.

In each of the high influence cases, the CPO also had high access to either the CEOs or another high executive's office. For instance, in Case J, influence increased when a new vice president of purchasing was named who had access to the CEO's office. Even though the CPO in Case M reported to another vice president, he had easy access to the CEO's office. This also was the situation in Case S. However, in Case B, the CPO held a high position on the organization chart but did not have easy access to the CEO's office.

The conclusion is that the formal position in the organization chart is not the important condition for influence. Rather, the important condition is the CPO's visibility throughout the organization and the access the CPO has to the top executive office. This leads to the conclusion that CPOs should be more concerned with their accessibility to the CEO's office and visibility through the company than with their formal position on the organization chart.

SUMMARY

Research consisting of 21 in-depth case studies of 24 organizations, numerous discussions with purchasing managers, and a review of the related literature, indicates that seven conditions create influence for purchasing in corporate strategic planning. A model was developed as a result of this research and presented as Figure 1. *Proactive purchasing management* is the central condition in the model. *Proactive purchasing management* involves forward-looking initiatives that add value and increase quality for the firm's products and services while managing costs. Specific initiatives may include managing total costs, involving purchasing early in the product and process design, including suppliers early in new product and process development, developing long-term supplier-buyer alliances, outsourcing, and involving purchasing in activities other than traditional purchasing.

Six conditions are preliminary to effective *proactive purchasing management*. The first two conditions are highly interrelated; consequently, a bidirectional arrow is placed between these two conditions. The conditions are the nature of the competitive environment and the extent to which executive leadership perceives purchasing as a process that can strengthen the firm's competitive posture. The research indicates that when competition increases and the top executives believe purchasing can improve the firm's posture, purchasing will receive increased influence.

However, purchasing leadership must take advantage of the opportunity presented by the executive leadership. Effective purchasing leaders have institutional commitment, possess a learning orientation, and have an understanding of the business. Each of these three conditions—competitive environment, executive leadership, and purchasing leadership—are placed on the top or the same side of *proactive purchasing management* because they are all highly interrelated and affect the extent of each other's impact.

The remaining three conditions are placed on the other side of *proactive purchasing management*. The first condition is *purchasing's congruence with corporate strategy and culture*. Purchasing strategy must be consistent with corporate strategy in order to support and implement corporate plans. In addition, purchasing culture must be consistent with the overall corporate culture in the norms, values, and beliefs that are demonstrated.

The next condition is *employee competence*. Purchasing management must either hire or train employees who are articulate, analytical, and assertive. These employees must understand the company's business and products, possess coalition-building and group skills, and be able to develop and use purchasing performance metrics. The final condition relates to purchasing and organizational structure. A loose-tight purchasing structure leads to the most purchasing influence. Purchasing influence is greater when the chief purchasing officer's visibility is high throughout the organization and the CPO has easy access to the CEO's office. Each of these conditions are more important than the CPO's formal position within the organizational structure.

REFERENCES

1 Shawn Tully, "Purchasing's New Muscle," *Fortune,* (February 30, 1995), pp. 75-80.

2 Jeffrey H. Dryer, "How Chrysler Created an American Keiretsu," *Harvard Business Review,* (July-August 1996), pp. 42-56.

3 Otis Port and Geoffrey Smith, "Quality: Special Report," *Business Week,* (November 30, 1992), pp. 66-75; Mike Doyle, "Strategic Purchasing Can Make or Break a Firm," *Electronic Business,* (March 20, 1989), pp. 46-48.

4 "Invoice? What's an Invoice?" *Business Week,* (June 10, 1996), pp. 110-112; "Jack Welch's Cyber-Czar," *Business Week, (*August 5, 1996), pp. 82-83.

5 Charles C. Poirier and Stephen E. Reiter, *Supply Chain Optimization,* (San Francisco: Berrett-Koehler Pub. 1996).

6 David N. Burt and Richard L. Pinkerton, *A Purchasing Manager's Guide to Strategic Proactive Procurement,* (New York: American Management Association, 1996).

7 Robin Cammish and Mark Keough, "A Strategic Role for Purchasing," *The McKinsey Quarterly,* no. 3 (1991), pp. 22-39.

8 U.S. Bureau of Census, *Annual Survey of Manufactures,* (Washington, D.C.: U.S. Government Printing Office, 1985), General Statistics for Industry Groups, p. 8 and appendix.

9 Charles A. Walts, Kee Young Kim, and Chan K. Hahn, "Linking Purchasing to Corporate Competitive Strategy," *International Journal of Purchasing and Materials Management,* vol. 31, no. 2 (Spring 1995), pp. 2-8.

10 Lisa M. Ellram and Amelia Carr, "Strategic Purchasing: A History and Review of the Literature," *International Journal of Purchasing and Materials Management,* vol. 30, no. 2 (Spring 1994), pp. 10-18.

11 W.A. Bales and H.F. Fearon, *CEOs'/Presidents' Perceptions and Expectations of the Purchasing Function* (Tempe, Arizona: Center for Advanced Purchasing Studies, 1993).

12 L.M. Ellram and J.N. Pearson, "The Role of the Purchasing Function: Toward Team Participation," *International Journal of Purchasing and Materials Management,* vol. 29, no. 3 (Summer 1993), pp. 2-9.

13 Walts, Kim, and Hahn, op. cit., p. 3.

14 J.L. Cavinato, "Purchasing Performance: What Makes the Magic," *Journal of Purchasing and Materials Management,* vol. 23, no. 3 (Fall 1987), pp. 10-16.

15 Henry Mintzberg, *Power in and Around Organizations,* (Englewood Cliffs, NJ: Prentice Hall, 1983); Jeffrey Pfeiffer, *Power in Organizations,* (Marshfield, MA: Pitman Publishing); John Kenneth Galbraith, *The Anatomy of Power* (Boston: Houghton Mifflin, 1983); Gary A. Yukl, *Leadership in Organizations,* 3rd ed. (Englewood Cliffs, NJ: Prentice Hall, 1994).

16 John W. Newstrom and Keith Davis, *Organizational Behavior: Human Behavior at Work,* (New York: McGraw-Hill, Inc., 1993), p. 55.

17 Robert B. Cialdini, *Influence: The Psychology of Persuasion,* (New York: Quill, 1993).

18 Robert W. Allen and Lyman W. Poerter (eds.), *Organizational Influence Processes* (Glenview, IL: Scott Foresman, 1983); Edmund R. Gray and Larry R. Smeltzer, *Management: The Competitive Edge* (New York: MacMillan, 1989), p. 16; James L. Gibson, John M. Ivancevich, and James H. Donnelly, Jr., *Organizations' Behavior, Structure and Process* (Homewood, IL: Irwin, 1991), p. 741.

19 Edmund R. Gray and Larry R. Smeltzer, *Management: The Competitive Edge* (New York: MacMillan, 1989), p. 16; James L. Gibson, John M. Ivancevich and James H. Donnelly, Jr., *Organizations', Behavior, Structure and Process,* (Homewood, IL: Irwin, 1991), p. 741.

20 Samuel C. Certo and J. Paul Peter, *Strategic Management,* 3rd ed. (Chicago: Irwin, 1995), p. 6.

21 Duane Davis and Robert M. Cosenza, *Business Research for Decision Making,* (Belmont, CA: Wadsworth), p. 30.

22 For a complete review of this literature see Amelia S. Carr, *Toward A Conceptual Understanding of the Influencing Factors of Strategic Purchasing,* (Ph.D. Dissertation, Arizona State University, 1996).

23 Larry R. Smeltzer and Sanjay Goel, "Sources of Purchasing Managers' Influence within the Organization," *International Journal of Purchasing and Materials Management,* vol. 31, no. 4 (Fall 1995), pp. 2-11.

24 E.G. Guba and Y.S. Lincoln, "Competing Paradigms in Qualitative Research," *Handbook of Qualitative Research,* N.K. Denzin and Y.S. Lincoln (eds.) (Thousand Oaks: SAGE, 1994), pp. 105-137.

25 Dilbert C. Miller, *Handbook of Research Design and Social Measurement,* 5th Ed. (Newbury Park, CA: 1991), p. 5.

26 D. Davis and R.M. Cosensa, *Business Research for Decision Making,* 3rd Ed. (Belmont, CA: Wadsworth Publishing Company, 1993), pp. 134-145.

27 F.N. Kerlinger, *Foundations of Behavioral Research* 2nd Ed. (New York: Holt, Rinehard, and Winston, 1973).

28 R.K. Yin, *Case Study Research: Design and Methods,* (Newbury Park, CA: SAGE, 1989).

29 B.M. Miles and A.M. Huberman, *Qualitative Data Analysis,* (Beverly Hills, CA: SAGE, 1984).

30 J.P. Goetz and M.D. Le Compte, "Ethnographic Research and the Problem of Data Reduction," *Anthropology Education Quarterly,* 12, (1981), pp. 51-70.

31 N.G. Fielding and J.L. Felding, *Linking Data,* (Beverly Hills, CA: SAGE, 1986).

32 R.G. Burges, *In the Field: An Introduction to Field Research,* (London: George Allen & Unwin, 1990).

33 R.E. Spekman and R. Hill, "Strategy for Effective Procurement in the 1980s," *Journal of Purchasing and Materials Management, vol.* 16, no. 4 (Winter 1980), pp. 2-7.

34 S. Rajagopoal and K.N. Bernard, "Strategic Procurement and Competitive Advantage," *International Journal of Purchasing and Materials Management, vol.* 29, no. 4 (Fall 1993), pp. 12-20.

35 M. Leenders and H. Fearon, *Purchasing and Materials Management,* (Burr Ridge, IL: Irwin, 1993).

36 S. Heinritz, P. Farrell, L. Giunipero, and M. Kolchin, *Purchasing: Principles and Applications,* 8th Ed. (Englewood Cliffs, NJ: Prentice-Hall, 1991).

37 Donald W. Dobler and David N. Burt, *Purchasing and Supply Management,* 6th Ed. (New York: McGraw Hill, 1995).

38 David N. Burt, *Proactive Procurement* (New York: Prentice-Hall, 1984).

39 Burt, op cit., p. 1.

40 David N. Burt and Richard L. Pinkerton, *A Purchasing Manager's Guide to Strategic Proactive Procurement, (*New York: AMACOM, 1996).

41 Burt and Pinkerton, op. cit., p. 1.

42 Carr, op. cit.

43 Carr, op. cit., p. 132.

44 M. Keough, "Buying Your Way to the Top," *Director,* (April 1994), p. 72-75.

45 V.T. Freeman and J.L. Cavinato, "Fitting Purchasing to the Strategic Firm: Frameworks, Processes, and Values," *Journal of Purchasing and Materials Management,* vol. 26, no. 1 (Winter 1990), pp. 6-10.

46 D.S. Ammer, "Top Management's View of the Purchasing Function," *Journal of Purchasing and Materials Management,* vol. 25, no. 1 (Summer 1989), pp. 16-21.

47 Smeltzer and Goel, op. cit.

48 Michael E. Porter, *Competitive Strategy: Techniques for Analyzing Industries and Competitors,* (New York: The Free Press, 1980).

49 Smeltzer and Goel, op. cit.

50 Peter Senge, *The Fifth Discipline: The Art and Practice of the Learning Organization,* (New York: Doubleday, 1990), p. 206.

51 James C. Collins and Jerry I. Porras, *Built to Last: Successful Habits of Visionary Companies,* (New York: Harper Collins, 1994).

52 Michael Miller and Laurie Hays, "Gerstner's Nonvision for IBM Raises a Management Issue," *The Wall Street Journal, (*July 29, 1993), pp. B1, B6.

53 Douglas Lavin, "Robert Easton Thinks 'Vision' is Overrated and He's Not Alone," *The Wall Street Journal, (*October 4, 1993), pp. A1, A8.

54 Gary Yukl and David D. VanFleet, "Theory and Research on Leadership in Organizations," in M.D. Dunnette and L.M. Hough (eds.) *Handbook of Industrial and Organizational Psychology,* vol. 3 (Palo Alto, CA: Consulting Psychologists Press, Inc., 1992), pp. 148-197.

55 Alvin J. Williams, "Supply Managers for the Twenty-First Century: The Learning Imperative," *International Journal of Purchasing and Materials Management,* vol. 31, no. 3 (Summer 1995), pp. 39-42.

[56] Shelley A. Kirkpatrick and Edwin A. Locke, "Leadership: Do Traits Matter?" *Academy of Management Executive,* (May 1991), pp. 48-60.

[57] Walts, Kim, and Hahn, op. cit.

[58] Freeman and Cavinato, op. cit.

[59] Robert F. Reck and Brian G. Long, "Purchasing: A Competitive Weapon," *Journal of Purchasing and Materials Management,* vol. 24, no. 3 (Fall 1988), pp. 2-8.

[60] Caron H. St. John and Scott T. Young, "The Strategic Consistency Between Purchasing and Production," *International Journal of Purchasing and Materials Management,* vol. 27 no. 2 (Spring 1991), pp. 15-20.

[61] W. Jack Duncan, "Organizational Culture: Getting a Fix on an Elusive Concept," *Academy of Management Executive,* 3 (1989), pp. 229-236.

[62] Egar H. Schein, "Organizational Culture," *American Psychologist,* vol. 10 (February 1990), pp. 9-19.

[63] Based on Daniel P. Denison, *Corporate Culture and Organizational Effectiveness,* (New York: John Wiley and Sons, 1990) pp. 11-15.

[64] Joseph R. Carter and Ram Narasimhan, "Is Purchasing Really Strategic?" *International Journal of Purchasing and Materials Management,* vol. 32, no. 1 (Winter 1996), pp. 20-28.

[65] Robert F. Reck, Robert Landeros, and David M. Lyth, "Integrated Supply Management: The Basis for Professional Development," *International Journal of Purchasing and Materials Management,* vol. 28, no. 3 (Summer 1992), pp. 12-18.

[66] Ellram and Pearson, op. cit.

[67] Joseph R. Carter and Ram Narasimhan, "A Comparison of North American and European Future Purchasing Trends," *International Journal of Purchasing and Materials Management,* vol. 32, no. 2 (Spring 1996), pp. 12-22.

[68] David J. Murphy and Michael E. Herberling, "A Framework for Purchasing and Integrated Product Teams," *International Journal of Purchasing and Materials Management,* vol. 32, no. 3 (Winter 1996), pp. 11-19; Shad Dowlatshahi, "Purchasings Role in a Concurrent Engineering Environment," *International Journal of Purchasing and Materials Management,* vol. 28, no. 1 (Summer 1992), pp. 21-25; Robert J. Trent and Robert M. Monczka, "Effective Cross-Functional Sourcing Teams: Critical Success Factors," *International Journal of Purchasing and Materials Management,* vol. 30, no. 4 (Fall 1994), pp. 2-11.

[69] Carter and Narasimhan, op. cit.

[70] Ellen J. Dummond, "Performance Measurement and Decision Making in a Purchasing Environment," *International Journal of Purchasing and Materials Management,* vol. 27, no. 2 (Spring 1991), pp. 21-31; Chiang-nan Chao, Eberhard E. Scheuing, and William A. Ruch, "Purchasing Performance Evaluation: An Investigation of Different Perspectives," *International Journal of Purchasing and Materials Management,* vol. 29, no. 3 (Summer 1993), pp. 32-39.

[71] Richard L. Daft, *Organization Theory and Design,* 5th Ed. (Minneapolis: West Publishing, 1995), p. 66.

[72] Michele Lui, Helene Denis Harvey Kolodny, and Benjt Stymne, "Organization and Design for Technological Change," *Human Relations,* 43 (January 1990), pp. 7-22; George P. Huber, "A Theory of the Effects of Advanced Information Technologies on Organizational Design, Intelligence and Decision Making," *Academy of Management Review,* 14 (1990), pp. 47-71.

[73] Thomas A. Stewart, "The Search for the Organization of Tomorrow," *Fortune,* (May 18, 1992), pp. 92-98.

APPENDIX A: SUMMARY OF CASE ANALYSES •

INTRODUCTION OF THE CASE SUMMARIES

Case research is designed to find important and common words, phrases, and themes relating to the research questions. This may emerge through interviews, document investigation, and general observations. Accordingly, each of the case summaries reports on some of the important themes that emerged during this research.

Case research results in a rich array of subtle information that can only be obtained by critical questions, keen observations, active listening, and accurate inferences. That is the advantage of the case research procedure. The disadvantage is that the case research information is frequently difficult to relate in a summary. Many of the nuances and subtleties cannot be thoroughly reported in the written format.

In addition to the problem of incompleteness, the information can be highly sensitive. Each of the following summaries have been disguised so that the company cannot be identified; however, every effort has been made to retain the important organizational dynamics. Only that information that has been deemed to be essential to the research question is reported.

Organizational Change

Although we read about change everyday in the business press, the full impact of organizational change was not appreciated until this study. Every case resulted in extensive descriptions of change throughout the industries represented, individual organizations, and the purchasing function. This was no doubt the dominant theme. Not only was it the main theme at the industry, organization, and group levels, the effect change has on individuals became apparent. Because change was such a dominant theme, it is only briefly mentioned in the following case summaries. It should suffice to say that each company involved was experiencing change at all levels.

Tense

The case information is generally presented in the past tense. Some of the analysis was conducted as much as nine months before the report was written. However, every case is a dynamic event for which it is difficult to establish a beginning and ending time.

Ratings

Purchasing's influence on corporate strategy was rated on a one-to-ten scale in which one is the lowest and 10 is the highest. The rating procedure is summarized in the research procedures section. The ratings are presented in this appendix.

**EXTENT OF PURCHASING'S INFLUENCE IN CORPORATE STRATEGIC PLANNING
RATING SUMMARIES ON THE ONE-TO-TEN SCALE**

SUMMARY OF MAJOR THEMES

This summary indicates the cases in which themes were especially strong. A theme may have emerged in a case but not been included here unless it was a dominant factor affecting purchasing's influence in corporate strategic planning.

Theme	*Cases*
Centralization/Decentralization of Purchasing	A, B, C, D, F, G, H, J, K, L, M, N, O, P, Q, U
Influence of New CEO	A, C, G, H, J, M, T
Changing Strategy	A, C, F, H, I, J, U
New CPO from Outside	B, I, J, K, L, M, N, O, Q, S, U
Corporate Reorganization	A, C, D, F, H, I, L, M, N, S, T
Outside Competitive Forces	A, D, H, I, J, K, L, M, P, T
Consultant Retained	D, H, L, S, T
Proactive Purchasing Management	
New Product Development Teams	A, B, G, H, J, N, T, U
Outsourcing	B, I, K, L, M, O, Q, U
Measurement	A, J, I, L, M, O, U
Partnerships with Suppliers	H, J, K, L, M, N, P, T, U
Increasing Corporate Expenses	D, U
Purchasing Leadership	B, D, N, O, P, Q, S, T
Employee Competence	A, B, C, E, M, N, O, P, S, T
Horizontal Influence	B, F, S
Purchasing Organization Structure	A, B, R
Management of Teams	A, C, D, E, F, H, J, N, P

CASE A: AEROSPACE

This $6.5 billion aerospace company had gone through major downsizing during the 1990s. This was similar to most other companies in the industry as a result of the governmental budget cuts of the 1980s. As an aerospace company, 99.9 percent of revenue involves government contracts, so much of its business depended on how successfully it responded to government RFPs.

Because of the tremendous reduction in governmental spending on aerospace projects, the company looked for alternative business opportunities during the early to mid 1990s. The company had made efforts to move into other markets; however, this had not been overly successful. Also, the company formed various types of partnerships with different companies in related industries in an attempt to move into new markets.

The company tried to find ways to develop efficiencies. After several stages of downsizing, the "surviving" employees admit that a sense of competitiveness was not present in the 1980s but a greater sense of urgency was present by the mid-1990s. As a result, much effort was expended to develop efficiencies. However, to quote one manager, "A government mindset exists which does not understand competitiveness." This perspective seriously hindered cultural changes. The attitude of many employees seemed to be that the company could do little about its own destiny. Many employees believed the future of the company was solely dependent on the wishes of outsiders rather than their own actions. Another problem was that the company was so large that it was having trouble making strategic and tactical changes.

At the time of this case, 80 percent of purchases were subsystems while the balance were capital equipment and MRO. The purchasing organization was responsible for procuring large and sophisticated subsystems. The company then assembled or integrated these subsystems. Because the company organized itself to respond to the bid proposal process, it frequently operated around proposal development teams.

Purchasing's Influence in Corporate Strategic Planning

Purchasing was highly influential in the planning process. Although there was no corporate vice president of purchasing, purchasing was highly involved in the core business planning. The purchasing function, although it reported to finance, wasn't perceived as less important than finance. A bid was not considered without the support of purchasing. Furthermore, the bid would not be completed without purchasing, and a purchasing professional might be the head of the bid team. This meant that purchasing had an integral role in the company's revenue generation.

Further influence was demonstrated by purchasing's involvement in key teams. Few critical cross-functional teams existed without the inclusion of a purchasing employee. On the one-to-ten scale, purchasing influence was rated an eight in this company's corporate strategic planning.

The following themes emerged during the case study. At times it was difficult to differentiate between the present and past because so much change had occurred. The following summarizes current themes which evolved from the past. The company is attempting to change or modernize these themes.

Industry

This industry possesses several significant differences that affect the purchasing process compared to other industries. As much as 80 percent of a major project was completed by subcontractors. These subcontractors were responsible for large, sophisticated subsystems critical to the project's success. Extensive value analysis and value engineering are completed early in the project. Without thorough analysis, it was not possible to develop a competitive proposal.

Success required interaction between sophisticated purchasing professionals and suppliers. Interaction is a critical link in the project. The interaction must be conducted early in the proposal process to ensure that the best design and value engineering is accomplished. According to one purchasing manager, the supplier of the major subsystem and the procurement managers must "hold hands throughout the project, from proposal stage to revisions, assembly and test flights."

This procurement process is much different from that in which the buyer sends out an RFB on a high volume, undifferentiated commodity. Much more technical expertise is required in the former situation. In addition, the ability to work closely with subcontractors, or suppliers is essential. This is why the purchasing professionals had such an important role in the proposal process in this company.

Early Involvement

The procurement team has always had early involvement with the proposal process. A purchasing or procurement member has headed up a major proposal team on several occasions. This is particularly interesting for our analysis. The company was engineering-focused but a purchasing professional—without a formal engineering background directed the all-important proposal team.

This early involvement extended to early supplier involvement. The company traditionally had engaged suppliers early in the bid process. The purchasing group believed it historically did this much sooner than traditional manufacturers. This is probably why purchasing had traditionally been seen as an important function within the company. Purchasing was the major conduit to the potential suppliers who were critical in the bidding process.

Organizational Structure

For many years, the company consisted of three major divisions organized along product lines. However, this was gradually changed because of the dramatic downsizing. One division began to dominate the other two divisions to the point where several managers speculated that the company would soon have one major division.

Purchasing Organizational Structure

Each division had a separate purchasing function and the three groups seldom talked to each other. But this changed when a new corporate vice president of operations was named. He organized purchasing so that there was one centralized corporate staff. Some employees referred to this as a "mega purchasing group," but in reality it was only about 25 percent larger than the largest previous purchasing function.

This reorganization gave the chief purchasing officer much greater clout because now all purchasing was ultimately responsible to one office. All policies and procedures could now be centralized. In particular, the systems for developing contract terms and conditions were all systematized. Furthermore, the reorganization allowed the CPO to develop an economy of scale for technical support systems. Probably the most important change was that a purchasing council was established. This council was responsible for *all* outside contracting. For instance, an outside contract by the information systems function had to be approved by someone on the council.

The purpose of the council was not to leverage the purchasing power. It wasn't looking for a common product group. This is understandable given that the company primarily purchased systems components. The council was looking most at tactical issues such as credit cards and MBE supplier issues. But the main outcome was that the council resulted in much greater organizational influence for purchasing.

Related to organizational structure was purchasing's contribution to teams throughout the organization. Approximately five years ago, the company began an initiative termed *Integrated Product and Process Teams*. This was an effort to develop cross-functional teams to look at efficiencies in both processes and product design.

As a result, purchasing professionals were assigned to many different teams; however, purchasing was different from most other functions because it would be assigned to teams on a temporary, full-time basis. Although the purchasing person reported to a purchasing manager, he or she would work full-time on a product design team or a process reengineering team. This meant that purchasing had an opportunity to exert influence in many different areas within the company.

Internal Leadership

A new position was created approximately three years ago: senior vice president of operations. This person was responsible for all operations across all three divisions. The person who filled the position was an engineer within the company for more than 20 years and had no previous formal purchasing experience.

The new vice president initiated two actions that greatly affected purchasing's influence. First, he centralized all purchasing operations under one person. This person was one of the most senior purchasing employees and was highly regarded throughout the company. At first some purchasing professionals saw this as a threat, but it quickly became obvious that it increased the function's influence. The second event was to establish the purchasing council. The vice president made a major presentation at the first council meeting stating its importance. The vice president made it appear that it was the initiative of the new chief purchasing officer, but in reality the council was "suggested" by the vice president. The vice president's presentation at the first council meeting gave the stamp of approval from the new COO on the initiative established by the CPO.

Two new positions and a reorganization resulted in greater influence for the purchasing function.

Competent Individuals

The company traditionally employed well-qualified purchasing employees. This was necessitated by the sophisticated cost analysis required for proposal preparation. Because the purchasing professionals were well qualified, they traditionally seemed to be respected and included in major decision processes. Although they generally did not have formal engineering education, they had extensive technical product knowledge.

Benchmarking

The purchasing managers believed that they were an early leader in internal benchmarking. While preparing proposals, they kept extensive records. Part of the benchmarking was the result of governmental regulations, but

it also allowed them to begin benchmarking their internal processes. This feature should be considered in combination with centralization because both contributed to influence. Benchmarking allowed them to ultimately measure productivity with something other than dollars. During the past five years, many different and creative attempts have been made to develop metrics, and because of centralization, the metrics made a major impact on purchasing influence.

These metrics allowed purchasing to provide executive management with solid measures when downsizing was occurring. Purchasing made a solid case that they were adding value to the corporation.

Increased Outsourcing

The company had always outsourced major components; however, outsourcing received even greater emphasis during the past five years. Due to economic pressures, the company stripped itself of everything but its core areas. As a result, purchasing became even more critical to the basic company functioning. This was one reason that purchasing did not experience the same proportion of layoffs as many other functions within the organization.

Summary

Purchasing had traditionally been respected within this company. This was largely due to the *industry*. Aerospace is significantly different from traditional manufacturing because it is bid-oriented rather than directed to product marketing. However, purchasing influence increased during downsizing. The major reasons for the increased influence was that a new vice president of operations gave greater attention to purchasing. Furthermore, economic changes required additional outsourcing and purchasing was integrally involved in this process. Essentially, purchasing became involved in a high-risk endeavor and gained influence because of this.

CASE B: NATURAL RESOURCE PROCESSING

This $3 billion company is divided into two major divisions. One division has a relatively homogeneous product line and accounts for slightly more than one half of the total corporate revenue. This division is headed by a president. The second division consists of a group of smaller autonomous business units. This second division generally consists of acquired companies that have retained relatively independent strategies under the control of separate presidents. The company has been going through many changes due to relatively poor-to-flat financial performance. Other companies throughout the industry have experienced similar problems during the past three to five years. The company largely had been a victim of world-wide conditions that affect demand for its product.

This is essentially a processing industry. The largest division is primarily responsible for processing raw materials. Purchasing is responsible for any materials used in the processing of the natural resource.

Purchasing's Influence in Corporate Strategic Planning

Several major changes occurred in the past three years that increased purchasing's influence. However, limited influence was demonstrated within the corporate structure as top management appeared rather indifferent to the purchasing process. The purchasing vice president was invited to the yearly management meeting for the top 100 executives. However, he wasn't invited to major planning meetings, and his ideas were not solicited.

On a more positive note, the new vice president had a background comparable to that of two other recently hired vice presidents. Also, he had relative freedom in pursuing his initiatives. But he was not asked to send much information upward. On the one-to-ten scale, purchasing influence in this company resulted in a rating of six. The following themes emerged in this interview.

Corporate Analysis

As is typical of most U.S. industries, this entire industry experienced severe competitive pressures during the past five years. Global competition was the primary source of competitive pressure. Financial results had been flat-to-negative, and stock prices had generally experienced a steady decline.

As a result of the financial position, the board ordered a complete corporate analysis. As part of this analysis, the corporation conducted a comprehensive, company-wide survey to determine what the employees considered the company's strengths and weaknesses.

The main finding was that the employees did not believe the company was doing many things as well as top management thought it was. Top management realized that some radical changes had to be made.

A special committee was established to look at many different company operations; purchasing was not included in the committee. The committee reviewed the purchasing operations as it did most operations.

Industry Dynamics

This is a natural resources processing industry for which the resources were contracted from 50 to 100 years ago. The core competency is the processing of these resources and then the sale of those resources to industrial markets as commodities. To remain competitive, the company must be able to process the materials in an efficient manner.

Purchasing was largely involved in what may be considered MRO. However, MRO was more important for this company than in most manufacturing companies because it represented a high portion of cost of goods sold. In addition, this was a major area in which the company could recognize cost savings. The natural resource that was processed had been acquired many years ago and that price could not change.

Also, the markets for the company's products were largely controlled through world supply and demand. Labor costs were largely controlled through labor contracts, which were renegotiated on a three- to five-year basis. A logical way to acquire cost savings was through MRO buys.

New Purchasing Leadership

A new person was hired as vice president of purchasing approximately six months before the company-wide survey. Several important points can be made about the new position. First, this was the first time the company had a vice president of purchasing. Second, the person was hired from the outside the organization. The individual came from an international firm that had an extremely strong reputation for its management practices. At about the time this person was hired, two other top executives joined the company from other organizations. One of these was a new position in marketing and another was a replacement for an individual who resigned.

The three new people all had some things in common: they were relatively young, had impressive backgrounds, and came from other well-respected organizations. Several people who had been with the company for a long time were asked why they believed a purchasing vice president was named. They believed that it was

simply something that was long overdue. It was not seen as a special endorsement for purchasing one way or the other. Most major functions had a vice president, so the establishment of this new position was due. Corporate leadership did not seem to be making any type of special statement with this new position.

The vice president believed that his charge was to bring many of the best purchasing practices to this firm. He did not believe that the executive group necessarily knew what best practices were; rather, it was his responsibility to determine what was best for the company and implement these practices. Accordingly, the vice president largely saw himself as a change agent. Not only was he to identify the best practices, his greatest challenge was to convince many others in the company — within and outside the purchasing function — to implement new practices. The vice president stated, "Sixty to 70 percent of my time is spent trying to sell ideas."

Organizational Structure

The vice president of purchasing was a divisional position rather than a corporate position. Although the vice president worked closely with the corporate finance and accounting people, it is interesting to note that the vice president was not a corporate position. But the corporate executives interviewed him before he was hired. The vice president had to work closely with the corporate people but no direct reporting relationship existed. In addition, he seemed to get little direction from the corporate staff. They generally did not ask him for information and his ideas were not solicited.

Although he had no direct relationship with the other division within the company, the vice president believed that much could be accomplished by working with the purchasing people from the various small business units within the other division. But anything that was accomplished had to be done through informal influence. This leads to the next theme.

Horizontal Influence

The vice president of purchasing emphasized that although he was a vice president, authority could not be used to get things accomplished. Rather, it was important to build coalitions. He used corporate credit cards as an example. He was working to get credit cards implemented in the large division where he was responsible for purchasing; however, he saw major advantages in convincing the other units to also use the cards.

At first, nobody, not even his own people, understood what he was trying to accomplish. Gradually, through selling his ideas, he was able to obtain the other units' interest. This enabled the corporate accounting function to establish some corporate-wide systems. Also, it greatly increased the vice president's influence outside his division. It generally increased purchasing's influence within the corporate staff.

Related to the credit card initiative were the efforts with leveraged buying outside of the division. Although the corporation was rather diversified outside his division, each business unit bought certain commodities that could be pooled. He also convinced the other units to look at families of goods. However, many of the smaller divisions operated rather autonomously, so it was a difficult task to influence them to even consider pooling their buying. He was also trying to encourage the purchasing employees to discontinue most bidding practices. As the purchasing vice president explained why he wanted to minimize bidding, he again explained why horizontal influence was so important.

The vice president stated that, as a result of his efforts, he was as much an educator as a purchasing professional. He was continually trying to find best practices that would work throughout the corporation and then selling others on using these practices. He firmly believed that if he could horizontally sell his ideas, it would be much easier to influence vertically. Results would speak vertically if he could implement best practices horizontally.

Employee Competence

The company and industry had gone through many changes. Were the purchasing employees ready to implement the necessary changes? Much training would be required, but more importantly, new attitudes would be needed. As the vice president stated, a much more proactive orientation would be necessary. Effective and efficient purchasing would have to be done in order for the company to remain in a competitive position. It was not clear that the employees could be empowered to take a proactive perspective. Would they be able to develop tactics so that purchasing would be capable of "adding value" rather than strictly completing transactions?

Besides the new vice president, only one person in the corporation had any training beyond an undergraduate degree. Only one person had earned the C.P.M. designation and that person was no longer involved in purchasing.

Besides a lack of formal training, the present group of purchasing employees seemed to have little knowledge about the state of current practices. They placed much emphasis on the clerical aspects of purchasing. For instance, bidding was of greater interest than was the possibility of establishing long-term, buyer-supplier relationships. Other than by the new vice president, little was said about attempts to reduce the supplier base or opportunities for EDI. It would seem that a shortage of both skills and knowledge existed.

Summary

Three major themes in this case are organizational structure, horizontal influence, and employee competence. Each of these are highly related. A strong belief was expressed that horizontal influence (or serving as a change agent) was an important role within the company. In turn, this allowed purchasing to demonstrate the influence it could have by implementing various initiatives such as credit cards and leveraged buying. Upward influence would be obtained by gaining influence in a horizontal manner.

The other theme was employee competence, which could be highly related to change. As things began to change quickly, the employees had to be able to implement a new set of initiatives. This would require both skills and knowledge, but the correct attitudes would be required also. It appeared uncertain whether the employees would have the correct attitude to adjust to the change and then be able to acquire the skills.

CASE C: ENGINEERING DESIGN

This organization is primarily a government contractor that experienced a difficult financial environment over the past several years. Its primary competency has been engineering design, but traditionally the company also had been involved in manufacturing and assembly. It has gone from being an $8 billion company five years ago to about half that revenue. In fact, major articles in *The Wall Street Journal* suggested that the firm would be purchased and possibly divested. Because of the financial environment throughout the industry, tremendous pressure had been exerted on the very core of the business. As a result, major strategic shifts have occurred in the past five years.

Purchasing's Influence in Corporate Strategic Planning

As the company took on a major strategic change, purchasing seemed to lose influence. The chief purchasing officer remained at the same level in the organization that was comparable to other functional heads. However, the function may have lost influence when teams became more prevalent. But the overall result of the team effort was difficult to determine. Also, the function was essentially decentralized even though the core process remained in the same department. Concurrent with this development, the CPO resigned and the replacement CPO was a much less senior person within the firm. On the one-to-ten scale, purchasing influence was about a four.

The impact of the strategic shift was the first major theme that appeared in this case study.

Strategic Shift

Just five years ago the company would have experienced liquidation or death if it would not have made some radical changes. As a result, everything was examined from the basic corporate mission and its products to the operational policies and procedures. Ultimately, more than 50 percent of the total workforce and one entire division were eliminated in the restructuring. But throughout this analysis, everyone agreed that the purchasing/materials management process was important. As the theme within the case emerged, however, it became obvious that the purchasing process may have become so embedded in other functions that it lost corporate identity and overall influence.

The main strategic change that occurred was that engineering design and assembly was to be emphasized. Previously, design was responsible for about 40 percent of the firm's activities, manufacturing about another 40 percent, and assembly about 20 percent. Now, manufacturing was to be completely de-emphasized and ultimately outsourced whenever possible. So that the organizational structure would fit the strategy, the company was completely reorganized.

Executive Leadership

As part of the strategic refocus, a new general manager was named approximately three years before this case. This is an important event for several reasons. First, this person had a strong engineering orientation with several advanced degrees in technical fields. Second, he had no experience with purchasing/materials management as most of his experience was in the technical design area. Third, one of the first things that he did was announce that he was going to centralize the purchasing/materials management function. He clearly indicated that his intention was to build a massive, centralized engineering design function and purchasing would work closely with this area.

At first, it seemed that the purchasing/materials management group would retain its original level in the hierarchy, and this ultimately was the case. However, it quickly became apparent the actual influence and the influence ascribed by the organizational chart were two different realities.

The reason that purchasing lost its influence was due to two events: outsourcing and integrated product teams.

Outsourcing

Because manufacturing was de-emphasized, it experienced a massive reduction in force. Along with these manufacturing employees went many of the purchasing employees who conducted the routine procurement function that supported manufacturing. Those employees who wrote the requests for proposals, evaluated the proposals, developed the contracts, and expedited the materials were no longer needed.

Meanwhile, the strategy was to outsource the major product components. The employees responsible for outsourcing were to have a strong product engineering expertise along with an understanding of supplier relationships and negotiations. Combined with the engineering expertise, a thorough knowledge of value analysis and value engineering was necessary. To quote one manager, "The make-versus-buy decision took on a new perspective. Within a year, it had a new meaning in this company." By this he simply meant that it was a buy decision.

Outsourcing and Risk

When discussing outsourcing, several purchasing employees mentioned risk. What would happen if purchasing failed to meet its outsourcing objectives? The function was at risk of losing credibility. During these discussions, it was helpful to think in terms of failure and delegation of responsibility or risk in the failure to meet responsibilities. Several employees stated that in the outsourcing model it was possible to directly identify the cause or source of failure: the supplier. In turn, the purchaser was responsible for the supplier relationship. In the manufacturing or assembly process, however, the cause of failure would probably be attributed to many different internal people because so many were involved.

Risk became a more important theme when discussing outsourcing. If an outsourcing failure occurred, one sourcing team, generally a rather small team, could be held responsible. Accordingly, a new model emerged. The sourcing team had to manage the supplier to reduce the probability of failure. In other words, the sourcing team must manage and reduce risk.

During this case it became obvious that the general manager had shifted the risk from the manufacturing process to the sourcing teams. He moved some of his better employees from the engineering groups to the sourcing groups. At first, employees could not understand why this was being done; however, during the case analysis it became more obvious why this procedure was being followed. It was possible to conduct only a short interview with the general manager. He did not discuss the re-organization in terms of risk but rather talked about taking advantage of the company's core competencies.

The general manager believed that the purchasing process was extremely important and he said, "Purchasing is critical to the company's new strategy." But he believed that procurement was an engineering function. Value engineering was the key to making the outsourcing effective. When asked about supplier relationships and the ability to develop long-term partnerships, he seemed to quickly change the subject. When the discussion came back a second time to supplier relationships, he mentioned that the legal department would take care of difficult contractual conditions as they occurred.

In a case study it is difficult to make concrete conclusions, but it seemed that the general manager, who was an engineer, saw the company strictly as an engineering process. Manufacturing was not a high priority for him. Furthermore, he did not understand the importance of supplier-buyer relationships.

Employee Competency

Purchasing took on a new role with the outsourcing emphasis. Was the traditional purchasing group ready to take on this responsibility? Yes and no. Some of the purchasing staff was eliminated in the reorganization while some engineering personnel were moved into purchasing. A new skill mix was required, but the "traditional" purchasing competencies lost importance. Extensive training was conducted for the engineers who were transferred into purchasing. It was definitely a case of engineers learning just enough about purchasing to survive. No doubt most of the employees viewed engineering as much more important than procurement.

An interesting comparison was made by a manager who said that an airplane pilot needed to know how the airplane operated but he did not need to be able to design it. Purchasing was to the design engineers as design engineering was to the pilots. The engineers thought they needed to know just enough about purchasing to "fly through their jobs."

As engineers became more involved in purchasing, the CPO resigned to take a chief purchasing officer position at another company. The person who replaced the CPO was a much less senior person with limited background. His total experience had been in the purchasing profession, and he was not educated as an engineer. Top management must have seen purchasing as a non-engineering function even though more engineers were becoming involved in the process.

Meanwhile, anyone involved with purchasing became much more involved in teams.

Teams

Outsourcing teams became an important element of the refocused organization. The general manager made it known that major outsourcing decisions would be made by teams. The teams were organized around product rather than process, so many different mixes of people became involved.

The traditional purchasing/materials management people believed that these teams would diffuse their influence and their fears became reality. Hypothetically, the purchasing personnel should have been in a position to become more influential because they were involved in critical decisions. However, their mix of experiences and skills was not compatible with what was now required.

Teams resulted in diffused responsibility. Meanwhile downsizing was costing many employees their jobs. Rather than gaining the required skills, many purchasing employees were competing for what they saw as the pure, traditional purchasing jobs. Unfortunately, these positions were largely MRO positions that still required the more traditional set of skills.

Summary

Three important observations can be made about this case. First, the environment within the industry required that a new corporate strategy be adopted. Second, a highly technical engineer took over the major executive position within the firm, and he had a different perspective for purchasing. Third, purchasing was not ready to capture opportunities to gain influence. Purchasing was not ready or able to manage the major risk associated with outsourcing. Outsourcing required procurement skills but the engineers believed this was only secondary to the procurement process. Purchasing as a function lost influence as the strategic refocusing occurred.

CASE D: NATURAL RESOURCE PROCESSING

This is a multi-billion-dollar processing operation that has a presence throughout the world. It has a long tradition of brand recognition. Its primary product is a natural resource commodity that is transformed into both consumer and industrial products. All together, it has more than 100 different but related products.

Like many companies in this industry, it has experienced much financial turbulence during the past two decades. Its stock performance has been above average for the industry but this industry does not have much glamour in the 1990s.

Because of the company's size, it has a large presence on Wall Street, so its performance receives much national attention. Also, it has operations in many foreign countries.

Purchasing's Influence in Corporate Strategic Planning

This is an extremely large corporation with many different operations. Accordingly, strategic planning is an extremely complex process. This makes it difficult to determine precisely how much influence purchasing has in the overall strategic process. Also, the organization has undergone some radical changes in the past two years. These two conditions made it difficult to determine the extent to which purchasing is included in the corporate strategic planning process. One measure, the CPO's position in the organization, indicated that purchasing was included in the strategic planning process. This individual was at the same level as other functional heads and was highly visible.

However, the function was decentralized. Also, the CPO resigned from the company during this case analysis and purchasing lost much of its perceived influence. Top management did not seem to understand purchasing's influence. It could be said that purchasing had not educated top management on the value that it was adding to the company. Accordingly, it is possible that the function ultimately did not have much influence in the corporate planning process. On the one-to-ten scale, purchasing influence in this company would be rated a six.

Following are the major themes that lead to the conclusion.

Executive Leadership

Approximately three years ago, the CEO made a major proclamation at the shareholders meeting which subsequently received much national press. He stated that the company's income would increase by 25 percent and the stock price would increase by nearly 60 percent in the next three years. Of course, this put tremendous pressure on the entire corporation, especially on the staff functions.

This theme may be seen as corporate leadership or it may be seen as external pressure because it may be said that the CEO was simply responding to what had to be done. The stock was languishing; published reports indicated the board was putting pressure on the CEO. Something dramatic had to be done.

To help carry out the CEO's proclamation, the company retained a major consulting firm to analyze the firm's performance and make recommendations to help meet its goals. The firm's first priority of business was to look at the organizational structure.

Organizational Structure

In the decade prior to the CEO's proclamation, the purchasing function was gradually centralized though the efforts of the purchasing vice president. Ultimately, 11 major areas reported to him. During this centralization, some major initiatives had been introduced in such areas as quality, measurements, and employee development. While these efforts were being implemented, gradual and steady efforts were made to reduce corporate-wide purchasing expenses. In particular, the department critically reviewed staffing levels and reduced headcount whenever possible.

The consulting firm believed that many good things were happening in the purchasing function; but, it immediately proclaimed that the headcount had to be reduced radically. This recommendation was made even though purchasing had been reducing its headcount more than other staff areas during the past three years. But the consultants maintained that for the corporation to meet its goal, expenses had to be reduced corporate-wide. Even though purchasing had made great progress, it could not be exempted from the reduction.

Along with the headcount reduction, the consulting firm recommended decentralization. This is an important point. It had taken a decade to gradually centralize the function and now the recommendation was to turn it in the opposite direction. Purchasing influence would be reduced if the function was totally decentralized. Purchasing's influence was weakened by an outside force, the consulting firm.

So why decentralize? The consultants believed that the purchasing department would get much closer to the internal customer if it were decentralized to the plant level. Some interesting political dynamics become apparent here. First, it could be seen why employees in some of the other functions, such as accounting and production, would like

40

purchasing to be decentralized—purchasing was grabbing too much power.

This perception seemed to be particularly prevalent among the production people. As purchasing became stronger in the organization, production was losing its flexibility. What the consulting firm failed to see was that purchasing was not getting closer to its customer as much as it was falling under the dominance of its customer at the plant level. Purchasing would not have the centralized clout for the political battles that would inevitably occur.

At any rate, the reorganization took place and many of the purchasing employees were assigned to production managers. A matrix, or "dotted line," organization resulted. Even though the employees reported to the purchasing function, they also were accountable to the plant manager.

Purchasing Leadership

Shortly after the reorganization was recommended, leadership went into a tailspin. The CPO who had been with the company for several decades resigned. A leadership vacuum resulted.

Purchasing did not lose its position in the centralized corporate hierarchy; however, the CPO's replacement was a nonpurchasing career person. In fact, the replacement had no previous purchasing experience. This meant that the new vice president had only limited understanding of the issues faced by the supply management people. Furthermore, the new person could not establish any new initiatives that would increase the function's value to the corporation.

This reorganization is highly related to the next theme.

Employee Competency

When the decentralization took place, the purchasing career ladder was taken away from many of the higher level purchasing managers. Imagine, first the vice president, who had been there for more than a decade, left the company and was replaced by a nonpurchasing professional. Then the function was decentralized, so many of the higher purchasing positions were eliminated.

The result was that many of the top purchasing professionals had their resumes on the street within several months of the reorganization. It was not long before the top executive group could see that they were losing their top-level purchasing expertise. At first, it did not seem that they cared about losing this expertise; but eventually the company was not able to fill key positions with experienced individuals. In addition, managers at the lower levels were also leaving the function because they believed it had lost its influence. In other words, the effect of the reorganization extended further than expected.

Proactive Purchasing Management

Prior to the reorganization, this company had a reputation as a leader in supply management. In particular, it had made efforts to reduce its supplier base before it was the common trend. Also, it had looked at some critical outsourcing decisions and began to develop buyer-supplier alliances. However, after the reorganization, the function was not in a position to become a leader in any proactive initiatives. In fact, several of the initiatives lapsed to an earlier level. For instance, several partnership initiatives that were developing, disintegrated with the reorganization.

The company was looking for ways to reduce expenses. However, some of the proactive efforts made by purchasing to reduce expenses were losing their momentum because of the reorganization. Looking at it another way, new efforts to reduce expenses stifled earlier initiatives to reduce expenses.

This contradiction could be interpreted in two ways. First, it could be said that the top executives did not understand what purchasing was attempting to do, so their efforts were not appreciated. Second, it is possible that purchasing did not have metrics in place that could be used to educate top management about purchasing cost-reduction efforts.

Teams

At the same time the company was going through the massive reorganization, it was implementing a commodity team approach. Many of the purchasing people believed they lost influence during this process. Why? Employees from other functions did not believe that purchasing brought much expertise to the teams; consequently, employees from other groups had greater influence on the teams.

The team effort was somewhat coincidental with the implementation of the *supply chain management* approach. Although it seemed that the company was generally just using this term, it presents an interesting possibility. As the *supply chain management* approach was implemented, the purchasing people may have lost observable influence because of the horizontal teams. If this were true, it would have been even more important for the purchasing group to bring expertise to the team.

Summary

The major themes are external influence, executive leadership, organizational structure, and employee competence in that order. A reorganization severely hinders the influence of the purchasing group. It is critical that the purchasing group be perceived as having influence, or a logical generalization is that reorganization can destroy previously established influence.

Another important point is that the reorganization does not necessarily have to be based on a rational approach. It is important to note that a consulting firm is generally retained to recommend changes. What if the consulting firm cannot find progressive changes to recommend within a function? The consultants will probably recommend changes anyway. This is why it is important that the purchasing group have extremely competent employees and initiatives in place so that purchasing can demonstrate its value to the organization. One conclusion from this case may be that employee competence is the most important prerequisite for organizational influence.

CASE E: HIGH-TECHNOLOGY MANUFACTURER

This specialized high-technology manufacturing company has annual revenues of approximately $750 million. The company has turned a relatively common material transformation process into a huge success because of its ability to adapt to a niche market. The company has two major facilities in the United States and one in Asia. It has experienced extremely fast growth over the past five years. In fact, it doubled its revenue in two years. Because of its tremendous growth, the company has had a difficult time hiring employees, developing facilities, and generally adapting procedures to the increasing company size.

Purchasing's Influence in Corporate Strategic Planning

The chief purchasing officer in this company did not hold a position comparable to other functional department heads. The CPO was not on the more important corporate committees such as the planning committee or what is termed the executive review committee. The CPO did not have the educational or experience background comparable to other department heads. In general, the purchasing employees were not as well qualified as personnel in other areas such as marketing and no special training budget had been allocated for these employees. The purchasing function had little influence in corporate strategic planning. On the one-to-ten scale, purchasing influence is rated a three.

Following are the major themes that emerged in this case.

Organizational Structure

The director of purchasing reported to the vice president of finance. The vice president of finance was on both the planning committee and the executive review committee. The planning committee met quarterly and reviewed all plans and the progress made on these plans. Following a monthly meeting, the executive review committee reviewed the total company operation. The director of purchasing had never attended a meeting for either of these groups.

Little interaction occurred between the director of purchasing and the vice president of finance. As the director stated, "He is a good person to work for because he leaves me alone to do my job." They generally met only once a month, at which time the director provided a general report on activities. Neither the CEO nor the vice president of finance had any direct experience in purchasing.

The company has three major manufacturing locations—two in the United States and one in Asia. The company was centralized among the various functions but the plants had relative autonomy. The various functions at the Asian facility reported to directors and vice presidents in the United States but close control was not maintained.

Purchasing Structure and Function

The director of purchasing was located within the corporate office, and the other purchasing employees were located at the manufacturing sites. The function was centralized, but a dotted-line relationship existed between the manufacturing manager and the purchasing manager at each of the three locations. Eleven professionals in three different locations were essentially responsible for all of purchasing. The responsibilities of the purchasing group were broken down approximately into 40 percent capital, 40 percent materials, and 20 percent MRO.

Capital acquisitions were generally seen as the most critical aspect of purchasing's function. The director of purchasing was a member of the capital acquisitions team. This team approved all aspects of the capital acquisitions including the selection of the supplier to be used. In many instances, only two or three suppliers existed for a piece of capital equipment.

With the approval of the capital expenditure, the purchasing group developed and negotiated the contract terms and conditions. The purchasing group did not believe it had the same level of technical knowledge as the engineering and production groups and was reluctant to make capital equipment recommendations to these groups.

When the purchasing employees were asked what value they added to the company, they said that it was their ability to be proactive. By proactive, they meant that it was important to begin action on a requisition prior to receiving the request from one of their internal clients. In short, they believed it was important to begin the paperwork early so that they could complete the order in a timely manner.

In many instances, the buyers believed that it was possible to know the capital acquisition committee's final decision before it was completed. This may be termed tactical proaction but not strategic proaction. An important point was that the purchasing group was not a major influence in the actual procurement decision; purchasing simply carried out the decision. In many instances purchasing did not select the supplier as this was done by committee.

The purchasing group believed they were proactive in the MRO area with the establishment of a credit card system. They had not yet selected a system but had established a task force to analyze options. An important note is that a person from accounting was the head of this task force. A credit card system was largely seen as a way to reduce administrative accounting procedures. It was not seen as a tactic to reduce the supplier base for MRO purchases.

Another area in which the purchasing people believed they added value was in their relationship with suppliers. They were the major liaison between the suppliers and the company. The purchasing employees all believed they were expert negotiators, and this was where they added their greatest value. Their goal or mission was to get the materials to the company with adequate lead time for a reasonable price.

Employee Competency

Purchasing employees generally had no plans for professional development. The director of purchasing received his college degree almost 30 years ago after he resigned from the military. His current top priority seemed to be retirement. Another senior purchasing employee was 58 years old and also discussed retirement options. One of the junior employees was working on the C.P.M. designation, but no one in the company had completed this certification program.

Within the past two years, three new people had joined the purchasing group. Two of these employees had been with the company in production capacities but neither had any purchasing background. The third was a recent college graduate who had not taken any courses in purchasing. In general, it could be said that the employees had limited knowledge about the best supply management practices.

Summary

This purchasing group did not have much influence in the organization, and it did not seem to be a major priority for them. The mix of employees may have been one of the reasons. Several senior people held the most important positions, and they seemed to be thinking of retirement more than proactive management. At the other extreme were several recent college graduates who were busy learning the business and had not had time to gain much internal credibility.

An interesting note, however, was that several of the younger purchasing employees were put on the important acquisition committee. One of them mentioned that it was important for him personally to learn much more about the product so that he would be able to make more of a contribution to capital acquisitions. The most senior employees, however, did not give any indication that this was important.

The CEO did nothing to make anyone believe that purchasing was important in this company. Several employees had been added to the function but, with the tremendous company growth, this would have been expected. The accounting and marketing departments had added more employees than purchasing. One reason the executive group may not have believed that purchasing was important was because of the type of materials purchased. The materials were generally available commodities, and capital acquisitions were completed by a committee.

The purchasing group did not take the initiative to implement any new programs. It could be said that it was actually slower at implementing a credit card program than many other companies and accounting was taking the lead.

This company's success was largely due to niche marketing of a unique product. The CEO was classified as a marketing whiz in several instances. The employees generally believed that marketing creativity was how the company would stay ahead. Production was not a highly complex process, and it was obvious that this was seen as being less important than marketing. Because of the industry, executives' orientation and the organizational structure, it is doubtful that purchasing will have much influence in this company. Also, the purchasing group was not predisposed to establish any initiatives that would increase its value to the company.

CASE F: MULTINATIONAL CONSTRUCTION COMPANY

This is a multinational company that focuses on design, procurement, and construction of large facilities. The organization has experienced double-digit growth while making a shift in emphasis during the past several years. Also, it has become involved in projects throughout the world rather than just in the United States. This shift was not unique to this organization as it was occurring throughout the industry.

Purchasing's Influence in Corporate Strategic Planning

Purchasing had typically been oriented toward MRO. It was not involved in purchase of critical items. When new positions were created, individuals with little or no purchasing experience filled them. The director of purchasing reported to the vice president of finance. The director had only limited influence over what occurred on the major projects. On the one-to-ten scale, purchasing influence was rated as a four.

The first two themes discussed below are highly interrelated.

Organizational Structure

For decades the company was basically organized around four major divisions. However, during the past several years it began to analyze its entire mission and objectives that resulted in a strategic change accompanied by a major reorganization. The most important aspect about the reorganization as it relates to purchasing was that it refocused the risk.

Before the shift in organizational strategy, the company was largely involved in the design of major projects and possibly some construction. With the shift, however, construction became a major focus. Now the company designed and purchased major systems and constructed an entire facility. Traditionally, purchasing was housed in a service division that purchased engineering design support equipment. This is what may be considered MRO for operations throughout the world. Purchasing conducted millions of dollars worth of transactions; however, it purchased largely noncritical items such as computers, office equipment, and so forth.

With the reorganization, the company moved into a much higher risk position. It is much more risky to procure major systems and construct a major facility than it is to simply design it. As the company moved into the higher risk position, procurement also had to move into this position. But many of the purchasing employees had a choice; they could have stayed with the services division or moved to the higher risk division of construction.

Risk

The reorganization brought to focus the whole concept of risk in relation to purchasing. In the services division, purchasing is in a relatively low-risk situation. Even though one buyer was responsible for some $30 million of product, it was not a high-risk purchase. These products were not going to help the company maximize its revenues to any large extent. But with the strategic change, the entire company was moving into a higher-risk position in order to maximize its revenues or rewards. Purchasing had to do the same.

The key phrase became management of risk. How does purchasing manage risk? Although the purchasing personnel did not directly mention the management of risk, the benchmarking, measuring, and lowering costs emerged when discussing purchasing activities in the construction division. It is important to note that the managers knew that they were moving into a new environment when going into these efforts.

As the company moved into construction, purchasing was becoming responsible for many more dollars. Their dollars of purchases would increase tenfold and the risk associated with the purchases would increase dramatically. Purchasing was in a position to obtain much more influence.

Everyone saw the importance of developing benchmarks and related measurements for their activities. The theme that emerged with this concept was continuous improvement. For purchasing to learn to manage risk, it has to be looking for continuous improvement. Accordingly, measurement was seen as a tool to monitor the function's improvement.

Several other interesting ideas emerged when discussing risk. First, the purchasing personnel did not see measurement as a way to obtain influence. They believed that results would speak for themselves and "proxies would not be needed." This is interesting because they may have believed that their measurements were only proxies. They believed that measurements were a tactic for gauging their own progress, but they did not see them as a way to gain influence.

Second, they did not see themselves as managing risk. For instance, when discussing long-term supplier contracts, they believed this was a way to reduce administrative costs. But herein lies a contradiction. The company was changing its entire focus to place more emphasis on a higher-risk business. Meanwhile, in their minds, purchasing was pursuing a cost-reduction strategy. Maybe it is a matter of semantics or mental set, but it would seem that the purchasing emphasis should be on the management of risk. Or stated another way, the purchasing orientation should be the same as that of the top executives.

When supplier contracts are extended, is purchasing reducing administrative costs or managing risk? Both. But the mental set of the purchasing people is important. If they believe they are reducing risks, they will look for different conditions in the contracts than if they are simply reducing administrative costs. In other words, the mental set of the purchasing people was not necessarily consistent with the corporate strategy...even if some of their actions were consistent. The conclusion is that if the group does not talk the same talk, it will obtain less internal influence.

Purchasing Structure and Leadership

With the strategic shift and reorganization, purchasing began to have a role in areas other than MRO. In particular, it was an important component of construction. A purchasing manager was assigned to each major project. This person had a dual reporting relationship to the corporate director of purchasing and the project manager. This is a logical reporting relationship but it defused purchasing's influence.

Purchasing was in a position to gain influence but decentralization minimized its gain. Leadership also hindered the opportunity to gain influence. A critical mistake could have been made. Four new purchasing managers were hired within a year for large construction projects. In each case, the project manager had primary impact on the decision and each time a project engineer was hired rather than a person with extensive purchasing experience.

Purchasing seemed to be a secondary consideration. Several of the purchasing employees previously involved with the services division transferred to construction; however, they apparently were primarily perceived as being responsible for transactions. Although positions were created with the purchasing title, people with a limited purchasing orientation occupied the positions.

Leadership did not pursue potential activities such as alliances. Leadership was more reactive than proactive.

Teams

The nature of work relationships changed quickly and dramatically as the company developed a new strategic focus. The two main characteristics were cross-functional teams and early design involvement. But to quote one purchasing manager, "It is important for us to get involved with teams in order to protect ourselves."

This obviously was not a proactive posture but, unfortunately, it was rather prevalent among the purchasing employees.

On the positive side, the purchasing employees are being asked to join design teams at early developmental stages. This would not have occurred two years ago, but generally, purchasing is seen as a critical part of the team.

Employee Competence

As the company began to look at a new focus, it was important that the purchasing employees developed a new set of skills. When asked what skills they possessed that added value to the company, negotiation skills was the most prevalent answer. To quote one purchasing employee, "We have a great deal more experience at negotiations than anyone else in the whole company. They should allow us to demonstrate our skills." Another employee stated, "If we get too involved in teams, we won't be able to use our negotiation skills." No doubt it is good to have the negotiation skills, but such quotes may also demonstrate that there was a lack of willingness to get involved in teams. A further investigation indicated that no special training was conducted for teams but all purchasing employees had attended at least one negotiation seminar.

If the appropriate group skills were not developed, it would seem that the purchasing people would not be able to use teams as a vehicle for gaining influence. Little interest in teams was expressed but at the same time this was becoming an important skill for all employees.

Summary

This organization had gone through a major strategic shift but it appears that purchasing had not gained much influence in the process. If purchasing was disposed to manage risk, it would have been in an excellent position to obtain more influence. However, the mental set of purchasing was not consistent with the firm's strategic orientation. Concurrently, the skill set did not seem to be moving in the same direction as the strategic changes. The CEO did not give special attention to the purchasing group and create an opportunity for them. However, it seemed that the strategic change within the firm was creating an opportunity for purchasing but nobody in leadership was taking advantage of it.

CASE G: CONSUMER PRODUCTS

As a consumer products company, this corporation has annual sales of approximately $4 billion. The company may be divided roughly into two major sectors. One sector generates approximately 45 percent of the company's revenues through sales of highly related product groups. The other sector represents approximately 55 percent of the corporation's revenues, but represents products and services relatively unrelated to the other division. Because the organizational structure is important to understand, this theme will be discussed first.

Purchasing's Influence in Corporate Strategic Planning

Purchasing was not highly visible in this company either in the related product or unrelated product sector. The function was not included in the formal planning process at the corporate or operational level. Little effort was being made to gain influence. No effort was being made to integrate the functions across operations in order to increase visibility. On the one-to-ten scale, purchasing's influence in corporate strategic planning was rated as a four.

Organizational Structure

For this discussion, one sector will be termed related consumer products and the other sector will be termed unrelated consumer products. It is important to note that the company did not label the two sectors this way. However, for our case study, it helps explain the differences.

The related consumer products sector largely developed as a core business. Over the decades, the corporation had largely been identified with these products which number over 100 variations of brand names. One president is in control of this entire group. Meanwhile, the unrelated consumer products is largely a result of acquisition. Many different presidents control the various operations within this sector. It represents approximately 15 different groups that are generally unrelated to each other. The only commonality among some of these groups is that they focus on the end consumer. Customer orientation rather than the product is the common theme.

The reason that the company diversified into the unrelated product group is that it is much more optimistic about market expansion in these product groups than the related products. The only way to increase business is through increased market share in the related products group. However, the market will likely increase for many of the products in the unrelated product areas.

The related product sector shared many functions such as purchasing, human resources, marketing research, advertising, financial services, accounting, and logistics. However, the various operations within the unrelated product sector were not integrated. Each company within this sector tended to be self-sustaining as few synergies among the different product lines had developed or been explored.

Purchasing and materials management remained somewhat decentralized within both sectors; however, it appeared that much more centralization could develop within the related product groups. The unrelated product sector appears to have had little commonality among them. The related product sector had a director of purchasing while the unrelated product sector had a number of different purchasing directors within the different operating groups. Within the related product sector, the director of purchasing reported to a senior vice president of operations. This senior vice president, in turn, reported to the president of the related product sector.

The director of purchasing was a corporate staff position. The purchasing/materials management personnel did not have a direct reporting line to the corporate position; rather, this was generally seen as a service position. The director of purchasing had four staff buyers reporting to him as they were largely responsible for commodities that could be used throughout the related product sector. Example commodities were sugar, packaging, and specialized chemicals.

In general, little effort had been made to centralize the purchasing process within the related product groups. Much of the purchasing was conducted at the operations levels within the manufacturing facilities. These facilities were located throughout the United States.

Most of the remaining discussion focuses on the related product sector.

Executive Leadership

The CEO held this leadership position for many years and was generally recognized as a leading executive in the consumer marketing industry. His acquisition of the various groups in the unrelated product sector had generally been seen as a positive strategy by Wall Street analysts. The stock appreciated nicely over the past decade.

The CEO generally did not focus on manufacturing operations, however. This obviously was neither his strength nor interest. During one product briefing, he did not understand why the commodity price had increased so dramatically. When told that an essential core chemical had risen over 70 percent in 18 months, his reaction was. "Find a new supplier...it can't be that difficult!" The manufacturing people attempted to tell him that a worldwide shortage existed but this explanation did not seem feasible to him.

Approximately three years ago the CEO named a new president of the related product group. This individual had worked up through the organization and had extensive experience in all aspects of the company including manufacturing, finance, and marketing. He had been a manufacturing manager earlier in his career; however, he had limited experience in the purchasing process.

One of the first things the new president did was to name a senior vice president of operations. This individual had a strong background in manufacturing but no experience in either materials or purchasing management. This new vice president made it clear that purchasing was doing an excellent job. A memo to the corporate purchasing group stated, "...maintain your levels of performance but continue to find new ways to cut costs." From this general statement, it may be concluded that little attention would be given to purchasing. Neither concrete nor challenging goals were presented to the purchasing group. The only purpose of the function was probably seen as buy at the right price.

In a subsequent meeting with the purchasing director, the senior vice president of operations indicated that purchasing was doing a fine job. Manufacturing operations had much higher priorities and purchasing would receive little attention in the near future. This proved true shortly after this meeting. A senior buyer retired and the director of purchasing wanted a replacement with extensive experience. A replacement with approximately only five years of experience was approved. In short, purchasing was not a high priority item.

Both the organizational structure and the executive leadership indicated that purchasing was not a high priority. Interesting points are that the executive leaders had little experience in purchasing and apparently little reason to emphasize the function.

During one of the interviews, a junior buyer within the related products group was asked if he would ever envision a vice president of purchasing within this company. His immediate response was, "Not until this executive management group changes. They don't understand the importance of purchasing and probably never will." Unfortunately, it also appeared that purchasing had no systematic plans for educating the executive group.

Industry Dynamics

As a consumer products company, the marketing department seemed to have top priority within the organization. Whenever a product was losing share or the market wasn't growing, the answer seemed to be to develop a new product or enter a new market. This marketing orientation did not seem to emphasize the materials within the product. The purchasing group was not included in new product development teams. However, a competitor demonstrated some interesting differences. This competitor had a cost strategy, (i.e., How can we develop the product at a lower cost than the competitors?) Accordingly, purchasing was involved in new product development and had much more influence within that organization.

The Competition

The most direct competitor would not allow a case study; however, some telephone conversations and analysis of secondary information revealed interesting information. First, this competitor was also a consumer marketing company. Manufacturing was much less emphasized than marketing, but several top executives had gone through manufacturing on their way to the top. But again, purchasing experience was essentially non-existent in the top management group.

The corporate staff, however, had a vice president of supply management who was at the same level as manufacturing in the corporate staff. But an important point must be made here. The corporate staff did not have much power in local operations. The local operations had a great deal of authority. Consequently, at the various manufacturing facilities purchasing had different levels of influence within the production facilities. In some operations, purchasing was part of the operation's executive group. However, in the case company, even within operations, purchasing was generally seen as the function that was responsible for transactions. It filled the orders.

The point is that the competitor was much different from the case company: purchasing generally had more influence in the competing organization. Even though it appeared that purchasing had much more influence within the competitor company, the most senior executives did not have any purchasing experience. What was the difference? The answer to this question leads to the next general theme found in the case.

Employee Competence

Both at the manufacturing facilities for the related products and the corporate staff, the professional backgrounds of the purchasing personnel could be questioned. Although most of them had college degrees, only two had degrees in business. Furthermore, only two employees had more than 10 years' experience in purchasing. These were the same two employees who had college degrees. The C.P.M. designation was not emphasized in the company, and evidence indicated that none of the employees with less than five years of experience were actively working toward the certification. In general, purchasing professionalism was not encouraged in the company.

Summary

Purchasing did not have high visibility in this company. Part of the reason could be that within this industry, marketing seemed to drive the strategies. In the organizational structure, the director of purchasing had limited exposure to the CEO. Also, the process was somewhat decentralized, which made it difficult to obtain influence through leveraged buys. Purchasing strategies that are generally considered proactive, such as early involvement in new product design, were not pervasive in this organization.

CASE H: TELECOMMUNICATIONS

This case involves one of the largest telecommunications companies in the United States Comparable to other companies in this industry, it has undergone extensive changes within the past five years. Even though the company had experienced tremendous change, or some would say turmoil, it has been one of the strongest financial performers in the industry. Both revenues and profits had increased over the past three years as the company steadily brought on new product lines through internal development.

Increased attention to competitive forces received almost compulsive attention. A major theme throughout the corporation had been cost savings. The CEO gave a direct mandate that each unit would reduce costs while increasing services and products. As a result, the company was able to increase productivity per employee by 20 percent over a five-year period.

As part of the competitive effort, the company completely reanalyzed its strategy and established a different set of priorities. To ensure that the corporation was in alignment with its strategy, there had been a major reorganization, and concurrently, a major reduction in force.

Purchasing's Influence in Corporate Strategic Planning

A vice president of purchasing managed a centralized process that had high visibility. The vice president was at the same level as the other functional heads and attended the executive management council. Although purchasing was centralized, the process was integrated with other processes via teams. In particular, it was included in new product development teams. On the one-to-ten scale, purchasing influence was rated as an eight.

Industrial Dynamics

The entire industry had been going through tremendous changes. Competitive forces emerged unlike anything in the history of the industry. The financial performance for most of the companies within the industry had been flat or negative. Something dramatic had to be done. Many new executives had entered the industry in an attempt to rectify the situation. This case company was no exception.

Executive Leadership

The CEO was named to this position just two years ago. He joined the company as the COO two years before he was named CEO. Prior to joining the company, he was the president of a much smaller company in the same industry.

The CEO had no experience in materials or purchasing management. However, everyone within the purchasing group believed he was quite familiar with the purchasing and materials management process. To quote the vice president of purchasing, "We were fortunate in that the new CEO did not have to be educated. For some reason he was extremely familiar with what we were trying to do and had to do." The vice president went on to say, "I always have the feeling that if we do our job he will appreciate the results. He believes in the importance of our function... What more can we ask for?"

As soon as the CEO took his new position, he announced three initiatives for the entire corporation: (1) reduce costs, (2) develop and implement new procedures that would bring new products to market more quickly, and (3) improve current products. Direct cost-saving challenges were presented to each unit or function. At the same time, he proclaimed that the corporation would be rethinking its overall strategy. No doubt existed throughout the company that major changes were about to take place.

A major consulting firm was retained to analyze the corporate strategy along with its organizational structure. As a result of the consultant's recommendations, major changes were made in strategy, organizational structure, and team emphasis.

Organizational Structure

The company's organizational structure included a variety of business units and a large corporate staff. The purchasing/materials management function was centralized within the corporate staff structure. The vice president of purchasing reported directly to the president. The vice president of purchasing was at the same level as the vice president of engineering and other functional departments. An executive management council met regularly to address corporate operating issues. The vice president of purchasing was on this management council. A separate council addressed major financial issues.

The vice president of purchasing had eight directors and two general managers reporting to him. The general mangers were responsible for services while each of the directors was responsible for a major supplier or class of suppliers.

Purchasing Strategy

Purchasing redefined its strategy as the company was reorganized. Emphasis was placed on customer service and commodity groups. Prior to this, purchasing generally waited for internal customers to take the initiative. The new strategy was to become more proactive and work with new product development or product changes early in the design stage. Purchasing wanted to be seen as a knowledge force that could add value. In order to accomplish this, it was necessary to be physically and psychologically closer to the internal customers. They believed that the way to become closer to the customers was to better understand customer needs. As a result, purchasing was generally involved with new product development teams.

The term *supply chain management* was adopted two years ago in order to communicate the change. Not everyone in the company understood this term, but the directors and vice president of purchasing believed that they were gradually educating the other functions. To quote one of the directors, "The directors would all probably agree that about 75 to 90 percent of our time is spent educating others in the company about our new strategy. But it seems that maybe about 25 percent of them are beginning to understand what we mean by supply chain management so we must be making progress."

Teams

Highly related to the organizational and purchasing structure was the emphasis on teams. The consulting firm that was mentioned earlier recommended much more of a team orientation throughout the company. Cross-functional teams became a major part of the company culture. This forced many of the functions to look at their processes differently, and some of them seemed to resist this introspection. However, purchasing generally viewed cross-functional teams as an opportunity to gain influence throughout the company.

The vice president first emphasized that it would be important for all purchasing employees to focus on team membership and skills. Everyone went through a series of meetings in which the team effort was discussed. A major theme in these meetings was that team membership would allow the purchasing personnel an opportunity to understand their customers and better serve them. In other words, a renewed effort on customer service occurred concurrent with the emphasis on cross-functional teams.

Training on cross-functional team membership was conducted by the human resources department; however, purchasing conducted additional training. Purchasing's training differed in that it emphasized customer service on teams as well as group dynamics. As a result of this training, the employees should not have had any doubt about the importance of cross-functional teams. To quote one employee, "Although it was never directly stated, we knew that if we didn't play the group game we possibly could be looking for another job."

While team membership was emphasized and the reorganization was occurring, purchasing management decided to begin to locate many purchasing personnel with engineering staff. Also, "trades" were made in which engineering staff members were exchanged with purchasing personnel for a short time. This cross training added emphasis to the importance of teaming and customer service.

Many purchasing employees mentioned the importance of breaking down walls or reducing the number of silos. No doubt this was on the minds of the purchasing personnel.

As a result of the teaming effort, most employees believed that they were being involved in new product development at a much earlier stage than in the past. Numerous examples were provided in which purchasing was now expected to be part of a team while just three years ago purchasing would not have been involved.

A quote from a purchasing director is important here: "It is not important to have a large number of people reporting to you or to have everyone under your thumb. The important thing is to get purchasing completed in a professional manner that adds value to the firm."

Employee Competence

Prior to the new CEO and the major changes that occurred at that time, the vice president of purchasing implemented a major initiative to improve the skills and knowledge of purchasing employees. This initiative followed two paths. First, a major effort was made to hire employees who had a technical background. The vice president believed this would increase purchasing's credibility throughout the firm. Second, major emphasis was placed on employee training. This training encompassed traditional purchasing skills as well as product knowledge.

Two special themes ran through much of the training: understanding customer needs and making commitments to the customers. It was believed that if purchasing could make commitments and follow up on them, credibility would be gained.

While the training was being conducted, a major reduction in force occurred. This provided purchasing the opportunity to remove those employees who were not committed to customer service and did not want to learn the requisite skills. Employees who did not adjust to the cross-functional team approach or could not obtain the correct skill level were also released. But top management allowed purchasing to replace many of the terminated employees. Analytical and human relation skills received equal emphasis in the search for new employees.

Purchasing employees generally believed that their unique competency was the development and management of suppliers. They generally believed in alliance development, so it was essential that they have a thorough understanding of negotiations as they relate to partnering.

Summary

Much had occurred in this organization that resulted in increased purchasing influence. Outside industrial forces and a new CEO no doubt were the primary change agents. But it is important to note that the CEO had no previous experience in purchasing/materials management.

Concurrent with the new CEO was the reorganization that emphasized teams. However, the vice president of purchasing and directors of purchasing were ready to take advantage of the situation. They were already centralized and had several important initiatives in place. It is important to note that prior to the new CEO, purchasing had already begun a program to better train employees. In general, it could be said that industry forces and corporate leadership presented an opportunity, and purchasing was ready to take advantage of it. Some highly knowledgeable purchasing personnel had already begun some proactive initiatives and saw the opportunity to take advantage of the team efforts to enhance purchasing's influence. But the opportunity to hire new, young employees who had no preconceptions was also important. Again, purchasing was ready to take advantage of a situation.

CASE I: CONSUMER PRODUCTS

Small gifts and related consumer items are the main products for this company. With annual revenues in excess of $1 billion, the company designs, produces, and markets gifts. These gifts have a strong brand identity and have been a solid producer for a number of years. In addition to its own products, the company purchases and markets other related gift items.

This company has a long, rich history and the largest market share in its industry. As is the case with most U.S. corporations, however, this firm has experienced strong global competition as well as tremendous pressures from domestic competitors. This has forced the company to put much more stress on cost containment and new product development. In addition, it has had to rethink its strategy. As a result, the company has experienced as much change during the past two years as at anytime in its long history.

Purchasing's Influence in Corporate Strategic Planning

The company recently named a vice president of purchasing, and purchasing became involved in an expanded critical process: outsourcing. Also, the supply chain concept was introduced and purchasing was a major part of it. On the one-to-ten scale, purchasing influence was rated at an eight.

Organizational Structure

The company was generally organized along three groups: product design, production, and merchandising. The terms product design and manufacturing generally explained the functions and processes they represented. However, the company merchandised products it did not design or produce; consequently, merchandising was involved with the retail sales of products the company produces as well as products designed and produced by other companies.

A large corporate staff serviced the three main divisions in the corporation. Accordingly, purchasing was centralized in the corporate staff.

Purchasing Structure

Over the years, purchasing reported to a variety of different functions from marketing and product development to operations. This company went through a major reorganization shortly before this case analysis. In the latest reorganization, a vice president of purchasing was named. This is the first time that this position existed within the company. The vice president of purchasing and the vice president of manufacturing were at the same level, and both reported to the senior vice president of operations.

A number of different people at a variety of levels believed that a vice president of effective purchasing practices was required to reduce cost because cost pressures were making a significant impact on the company's profits. It seemed logical that purchasing should be the function that had a primary responsibility to reduce costs. Over the past several years, manufacturing had been seen as the area in which costs could be reduced; therefore, various cost-reduction programs had been initiated within manufacturing. The next thing to do was to look at purchasing.

Although the company was being reorganized in a number of different areas when the vice president of purchasing was named, this was the only new position at that executive level. Also, no other new executive level managers had been named during the subsequent three years. As a result, it may be concluded that new executive leadership did not create this change; rather, the leadership must have gradually seen the importance of purchasing. The chief operating officer said the position was created because of an "obvious need."

The employees who report to the purchasing directors were not necessarily physically located near the directors. Rather, they were frequently located with the product design or manufacturing groups. This organizational structure was instituted several years ago so that purchasing could be closer to the customer.

Corporate Leadership

No dramatic changes in executive leadership had taken place over the past five years. Why did the COO suddenly believe that a vice president of purchasing was important? As mentioned earlier, he simply said that it was obvious that such a position should exist. But the actual reason could not be determined.

Another important point is that nobody currently employed within the company had the requisite background for the position. An executive search firm had been contracted to find a suitable candidate for the position.

A review of the present purchasing directors' capabilities within the firm indicated that none of these individuals had qualifications comparable to the other vice presidents. The major point is that the top leadership saw the importance of a new position whereas they did not believe the position was important before. Furthermore, top management had not been grooming someone for this position. A change in corporate strategy may shed some light on the situation.

Change in Corporate Strategy

The company had been experiencing greater competitive pressures during the past several years than it ever had during its long history. The company's products had traditionally been market leaders, and product quality and creative design usually kept it beyond the reach of competitors. But this had changed.

The company adapted two initiatives to meet the competitive forces. First, it took on a zealous cost-cutting program so that it could maintain its quality while being price competitive. Second, it broadened the product mix that it could merchandise. The decision was to buy many of the products in its new mix rather than produce them because some of the products deviated from the company's manufacturing capabilities.

Make-versus-buy decisions had to be made for a number of different products. Purchasing was integrally involved with these decisions. Also, purchasing became heavily involved in the outsourcing process. By the time the new position was announced, approximately two-thirds of purchasing's efforts were directed toward outsourcing processes. This change had evolved over a period of approximately three years. Some of the most highly qualified and experienced purchasing employees were involved with outsourcing rather than with activities that were considered traditional purchasing within the company. But this was a new area for even the most qualified purchasing professionals.

As the corporate strategy was changing, the term "supply chain" began to emerge. This term was initially introduced by the manufacturing vice president, but it also included the make-versus-buy decisions. The supply function took on a much broader connotation than purchasing.

During a telephone conversation, the COO was asked what was meant by supply chain. He replied, "The supply chain includes any process that brings any materials or services into this company and puts them on the shelf at the point of merchandising. We want to look at things differently than we did in the past. We want to look at how we can add value in the supply chain."

In other words, the supply process was taking a much broader perspective in this company than it had prior to the strategic change, and the make-versus-buy decision was considered part of the supply chain.

This change in corporate strategy could have been the reason that the need was seen for a vice president of purchasing. No doubt this position was going to give the function increased influence within the firm. However, it may also be said that the change in corporate strategy is what actually added to the function's influence.

Supply Strategy

Purchasing was traditionally rather routine and reactive in this company. However, concurrent with changes in corporate strategy, purchasing was attempting several strategic changes. First, purchasing was trying to move more of the routine tasks to automation with tactics such as credit card procurement. Second, purchasing was trying to organize around commodities rather than product lines, so leveraged buys would be possible. Purchasing was also attempting to reduce the supplier base and develop several long-term alliances. Unfortunately, these efforts were not moving as fast as the purchasing directors would have liked. One of the problems was that purchasing employees' momentum slowed when it became known that a new vice president would be named. Once the vice president was named, each of these efforts increased in intensity. Also, purchasing became extensively involved in the outsourcing process.

Employee Competence

The traditional buyer within the company was not required to have a college degree, and obtaining the C.P.M. designation was encouraged but not strongly. Experience with the product line was given priority over a college degree when it was time to fill a purchasing position. It was considered more critical that the person understand the issues faced within the business than understand the purchasing process.

This orientation was causing some problems. First, on several occasions it was necessary to go outside the company to fill key positions because no purchasing career track had been developed. Second, no purchasing expertise existed for dealing with make-versus-buy decisions and outsourcing in a number of instances.

Summary

In this case, the corporate strategy seemed to affect the potential influence of the purchasing process. But it may be said that the change in corporate strategy was a result of industrial pressures. New competition was forcing the company to revisit its basic strategy. In turn, the correct organizational structure and personnel were not in place to implement the strategy.

The new organizational structure and new purchasing leadership gave the purchasing function much greater influence. But two problems existed. First, employee competencies were not at the necessary level to implement the new strategy. Expertise would have to be increased. If appropriate expertise is not available to carry out the plan, failures or mistakes may erode purchasing's influence and credibility.

The second problem was that the present purchasing strategies were not totally consistent with the new corporate strategies. Priorities must change, and this may demoralize the directors who had begun these initiatives. Many present employees would have to be refocused, and extensive training would be necessary for current or new employees added to the purchasing group. If the present situation continued, the purchasing function would probably not have credibility or influence with the other parts of the organization.

The key to this case was that outscoring was initiated about three years ago. The value analysis and long-term agreements associated with outsourcing required a different set of competencies than the purchasing traditionally done in this organization. This outsourcing would increase purchasing influence, but potential failures that could erode influence also existed.

CASE J: NATURAL RESOURCE/MINING

This case involves a $7-billion corporation that, for decades, was strictly involved with mining. Over the past decade, however, it has diversified into both related and unrelated products. The primary reason the company diversified was that the minerals it mined were susceptible to world price fluctuations that had been depressed over the past several years. Over the past decade, an abundance of product had been on the market; consequently, no matter what the company did, it was not going to experience a large profit margin. It could do nothing to affect product price.

The company had been able to accumulate a large cash reserve. The five years prior to this case analysis, the company used the cash for acquisitions of other businesses. Some of the acquisitions had been in highly related product lines while others were rather unrelated. Although mining remained the company's core business, during the past several years much attention had been focused on the new acquisitions.

Purchasing's Influence in Corporate Strategic Planning

A new position was created — vice president of purchasing — and given control over all procurement activities. Concurrently, a strong cost-reduction effort was initiated. This gave purchasing an important role. The purchasing function within any acquired business unit was part of a corporate purchasing council. This centralization gave purchasing increased influence. The CEO provided extensive support to the purchasing function. On the one-to-ten scale, purchasing influence was rated a nine.

The following themes emerged from this case study.

Industrial Dynamics

This company had existed since the turn of the century, and for the first 80 years little had changed. Of course economic ebbs and flows occurred, but the company was generally able to wait out the cycles and return to a strong position. However, the world economy that created new competition for its product in the 1980s appeared to change the industry's stability.

In 1990 the company was in one of its longest and deepest negative cycles largely due to overcapacity and a weak demand. Several smaller companies in the industry were closed and the larger ones had to make radical changes. This case company was a large force in the industry but was having the same problems as the others companies. Changes had to be made.

Corporate Executive Leadership

In 1990 the CEO "retired" at an early age. The majority of people interviewed for this case study believed that strong pressure was placed on the former CEO to retire. The retired CEO had spent his entire career in the mining industry moving through operations, finance, and marketing to the top position. The new CEO had quite a different background. He had a Ph.D. in economics and had served on many national policy-making boards and commissions. He knew little about mining; his expertise was in industrial economics.

The first thing the new CEO did was to say that he wanted the mining operation to reduce costs every year over the next five years. He established rigorous goals for each mining site and corporate function. Next, he announced that the company wanted to acquire companies in related industries. He made it clear that any acquisition would not remain autonomous. He wanted to develop an employee expertise within the corporate staff that would better manage the acquisitions.

The new CEO also made it obvious that he was going to "manage by the numbers." By this he meant that he wanted to establish goals and have results reported in concrete numbers. It was obvious to the purchasing group that he was an economist, and measurement was important to him.

Organizational Structure

Prior to the arrival of the new CEO, the purchasing function had a director who reported to the vice president of operations. Although it was difficult to determine because of the timing of the case study, it appeared that the purchasing function had been a rather traditional, reactive function. It was not involved in any corporate decision-making prior to 1990.

By 1992 a corporate staff was established that had much greater power than the staff prior to 1990. One member of this staff was a vice president of purchasing who had an advanced degree in business and more than 20 years of experience in mining operations. Most important, this individual also had experience in a manufacturing facility as a purchasing manager. He was hired from a competing company.

The new vice president of purchasing was given clear control of all purchasing functions within the corporation. He was included in all acquisition decisions and his recommendations seemed to be important. It was made clear that any purchasing functions within an acquired company would initially have at least an informal relationship with the vice president. But total control would evolve rather quickly to the vice president of purchasing.

The vice president had four directors reporting to him. These directors were generally responsible for the mining operations at the various locations. However, the vice president also had a general manager responsible for special operations and another general manager responsible for new projects. Both of these general managers had a high level of authority and generally had more influence than the directors.

Purchasing Strategy

Prior to 1992, purchasing was conducted in a rather reactive manner. The buyer received requisitions and completed the order, usually through a bidding process. The purchasing process was the same regardless of the material or capital equipment involved. A rather standardized, routine process was followed. After 1992, the purchasing strategy included both the mining operations and the new units acquired through acquisitions.

The major initiative was the establishment of a purchasing council. The purpose of the purchasing council was to develop initiatives that would reduce costs throughout the corporation, including the costs of new acquisitions. Previously the various locations had operated rather autonomously, but it was made clear that this would not continue. The council was able to develop strategies for leveraged buying and major cost reductions. A representative of each newly acquired company was included in the council. The council was the controlling entity of the purchasing function, and all units were required to follow the initiatives established by this group. The CEO periodically attended the council meetings to assure that the proper perspective was placed on its importance.

The vice president made it clear that he wanted to replace any routine purchasing activities with information systems. He also placed extensive emphasis on leverage buys, reduction of the supplier base and forming long-term alliances. In other words, he was attempting to make this a best-in-class purchasing operation.

Employee Competency

More than half of the purchasing employees present in 1990 were no longer with the company in 1995. Much of the reduction was accomplished with retirements and voluntary separations, but a number of involuntary separations also occurred. In addition, the purchasing employees in the acquired business units were told that purchasing would be accomplished consistent with the corporate philosophy and strategy. Many changes would be expected. This resulted in a high turnover within the newly acquired businesses.

Replacements were generally new college graduates or employees with less than five years of experience.

This allowed the new vice president to quickly assimilate the new staff to his way of business. But it also meant that purchasing had limited expertise. The same process was occurring in other functions throughout the company so purchasing was not seen as a deviation from the norm.

The newer employees were much more quantitative than the older group of employees. The CEO's philosophy of managing by the numbers was much easier to accomplish with this group because they had the quantitative and computer skills required. In addition, they had the human relations skills required to infuse their way of doing business throughout the other functions.

Internal Coalition Building

Between 1992 and 1995, two new purchasing directors had replaced one who retired and one who resigned. Both of these directors had come from companies outside the industry that were generally considered progressive organizations. These two new directors were both aggressive and brought a number of new ideas about the way to manage the supply process.

In an interview, a director stated that he was essentially a change agent. His skills and knowledge in purchasing were not being challenged as much as his ability to introduce change. This change was within his own staff as well as other functions. He said, "What I really need is a good seminar on selling...I am continually trying to sell people on the best way of doing things. Or maybe it is a matter of education. Whatever it is, it is a definite challenge." A similar sentiment was echoed by the other new director who said, "So many of our people are not familiar with current practices that I am continually educating them."

The education or selling process was largely accomplished by getting good employees placed on critical task forces or cross-functional teams. The vice president and directors worked hard to get the most knowledgeable and articulate people on these teams. This was especially true in the newer business units. On two occasions they transferred employees from the mining division to a newly acquired business unit. When asked about the purpose of this transfer, the director said, "To spread the procurement gospel." Within just a matter of several years, purchasing employees were asked to join important teams for which they would not have been considered before.

A Cultural Change: Teams

The entire company was undergoing tremendous cultural changes in a matter of several years. "Change was a constant." A new sense of competitiveness was instilled within every function. Strategies for cost savings were a theme in most meetings.

Part of the new culture was implemented through extensive use of teams. The normal departmental boundaries were reduced because there were several new vice presidents who emphasized collaboration across functional walls.

This culture of team efforts worked to the advantage of purchasing. It was now possible to get involved in processes in which purchasing employees formally had not been included. To quote one buyer who had been with the company for more than 10 years, "We are definitely invited to activities that we didn't even know about before. It seems that we have respect that in the past I didn't even knew existed."

Summary

Industrial dynamics forced the company into change. Meanwhile a highly aggressive CEO hired a new vice president of purchasing who immediately made a number of radical changes. The purchasing process immediately got the attention of top management because of the many changes that were taking place. Little of the change probably would have occurred from within the company without the new CEO and vice president.

The new management group developed influence by immediately bringing in a number of new employees who were rather assertive. The new employees quickly learned to manage by the numbers and developed a series of creative metrics from which they could benchmark their activities. The newer employees also emphasized internal influence by joining a number of groups throughout the company.

External pressures created change that resulted in greater internal influence. But many internal changes had to be made quickly in order to take advantage of the external forces. Part of the change was that many of the former employees were replaced by younger employees with limited experience. It was easier to teach them the new way of doing business. All of these changes resulted in much greater influence for purchasing in the corporate strategy development process.

CASE K: FINANCIAL SERVICES FIRM

A large national financial services firm is the focus of this case study. This entire industry experienced turmoil in the 1980s. But the industry, and this company specifically, is in a much stronger financial posture in the mid-1990s. The company has three basic approaches that it can use to increase its competitiveness. First, it can develop new creative financial products. This is generally difficult as regulations limit the product mix. Second, it can implement a more aggressive marketing program and develop a larger sales force. Again, it is a competitive industry in which marketing has been the major competitive weapon so this approach seems to have limitations. The third strategy is to reduce its administrative costs.

Purchasing's Influence in Corporate Strategic Planning

Although the ratio of purchases to total revenues is small in this firm compared to that of a manufacturing organization, purchasing's influence is rather high. The purchasing director has high visibility in the corporate office. Every tangible indication, such as offices, titles, education, and experience, along with position in the organizational structure indicates that he is at the same level as the other functional directors. The employees are well trained and have high visibility on major committees throughout the company. Also, the director is on the influential executive committee along with the director of marketing. Finally, the purchasing function became responsible for a major budget item that represented a variable cost. On the one-to-ten scale, influence is rated at a seven.

Following are the major themes that emerged in this case study.

Corporate Strategy

A financial services firm is heavily regulated on the type of products it can offer. In the tumultuous 1980s, regulation became even worse according to industry executives. Because of the tremendous competitiveness, many small firms were acquired by larger firms in the late 1980s and 1990s. Acquisition was this company's strategy. Certain economies of scale could be realized as the larger national firm acquired the smaller regional firms. The general strategy was to centralize operations as much as possible while allowing the regional firms to maintain their identity.

Gradually the regional firms took on the national firm's identity. Also, the corporate office quickly took over the information systems. It was common for staff positions in the regional offices to be offered corporate positions and relocate or face termination.

The entire industry was on an "acquisition binge," and soon there was not much more acquisition that could take place. The next move was to find new administrative efficiencies beyond simply centralization of functions.

Corporate Leadership

The executive leadership in this firm included several of the most respected individuals in the industry. The CEO had earned several awards for his creativity and leadership within the industry. He was generally seen as a creative leader rather than one who reacted to trends.

Purchasing Structure

Purchasing was centralized along with the other administrative functions as the acquisitions took place. Although there were a few purchasing professionals in the newly acquired operations, it was made clear to them that everything was to be centralized within one national office.

The purchasing director reported to the executive vice president of operations. In turn, this executive vice president reported directly to the CEO. The only other executive vice president position was in finance. Contrary to many financial service firms, this organization did not have many vice presidents at the corporate level so a director was high in the organizational chart. The purchasing director was allowed to operate the function rather autonomously.

Purchasing Leadership and Strategy

Four years ago, while the firm was involved in its "acquisition binge," it hired a new purchasing director. The director had served in a variety of positions in a manufacturing environment including marketing and industrial relations. He had never served as a purchasing manager and never had been in the financial services industry. This was a major change for him.

The executive vice president stated, "Change management is what this industry needs. We needed a manager who has a vision and understands management."

The director said, "I was hired to make cost-saving changes. Purchasing knowledge can be acquired but my asset is working with people to implement changes." Change was the theme in this case.

The first thing the new director did was to tell all of the purchasing employees that things were going to change. He went so far as to say, "I believe that change for change's sake is good. It gets us to look inside the bag, and a rabbit might be there and surprise all of us."

His main objective was to reduce expenses, so he established some challenging goals. The goals required the purchasing staff to look at their practices and find new ways to reduce costs. Primary initiatives were in developing long-term alliances, leveraging purchases and developing information systems — including credit cards — that would reduce administrative expenses. The motto was, "Do whatever it takes to reduce administrative expenses."

Surprisingly, risk became a theme in the strategy. In an effort to reduce their supplier base, they developed relationships with single suppliers. Also, purchasing began to look at outsourcing major administrative functions.

Outsourcing

One activity that was outsourced under the direction of purchasing was temporary employees. This was a major change and involved much risk for the purchasing group for several reasons. Before it can be explained why this was a high-risk endeavor for purchasing, it is important to explain more fully what occurred. The purchasing director was looking at all expenses in which purchasing had not been traditionally involved. Temporary employees were a major expense in which the director believed that one national contract could result in major savings.

Prior to discussing the issue with the human resource director, the purchasing director found several other companies that had national contracts for temporary employees and discussed how they arranged the contract. The director then developed a proposal and presented it to the executive vice president. In the proposal, the purchasing director emphasized what he believed were purchasing's primary competencies such as developing requests for proposals, analyzing bids, developing contracts, and maintaining supplier relationships. The proposal also included a corporate-wide implementation plan for hiring temporary employees. The proposal was adopted by the executive planning committee with little debate.

Why was this a high-risk endeavor for the purchasing director? First, expenditures for temporary employees were a major budget item. In regional offices and smaller branch offices, temporary employees often made up 30 percent to 40 percent of the total salary expense. Unfortunately, the percentage of expenses that this represented could not be obtained for this case analysis.

The second way it involved risk is that it was a major new area of involvement for purchasing. If the function failed on this endeavor, it would not have credibility in other areas. Third, the purchasing function was made responsible for a process that the human resource group traditionally saw as their area. The HR group simply got blind-sided, so it was a political risk for the purchasing group.

Within six months of implementing the new plan, everything was going smoothly. The marketing department initiated a discussion with the purchasing department about the process the marketing group used to acquire advertisements. The purchasing group was in the process of finding other purchasing groups that purchased advertisements. Purchasing had become a direct service to marketing in a nontraditional manner.

Employee Competency

When the purchasing director took over the new job, he immediately attended several workshops on purchasing and visited with a number of purchasing directors in comparable industries. Subsequently, he developed a rigorous plan for improving the purchasing competencies for each employee. Specific goals for professional development were established, and he appeared to be able to sell most employees on their importance. But he was also fortunate in that two of the most senior employees left the organizations shortly after he established the goals. This was fortunate in that these senior employees were probably seen as models of those who would not adopt the new way of thinking about purchasing. Not only would they now no longer be a barrier to a cultural change, it was clear to the remaining employees that they would either change or be asked to leave the organization.

Two new employees were hired at senior purchasing managerial levels. Both individuals came from dissimilar industries in which purchasing had a much higher profile. As they both became part of the purchasing director's senior management team, it was obvious that the employees who had long been with the group would be asked to stretch themselves in both skills and knowledge. In fact, the two new managers both encouraged the other employees to pursue professional certification. Prior to this, not one employee in the organization was a certified purchasing manager, but both of the new managers had earned their certification.

Organizational Politics

The new purchasing director was adamant that it was important to sell the worth of the purchasing process throughout the company. As he convinced his own staff of this, he encouraged them to look for new ways to measure their organizational impact. He tried to look beyond dollars. He was a big advocate of looking for proxy measures.

The purchasing group especially used organizational politics when selling the credit card program. Rather than just discussing savings, they emphasized convenience, employee empowerment and additional information about departmental expenses. In short, they emphasized benefits to other departments and de-emphasized the benefits for the purchasing groups. Concurrently, purchasing developed specific measurements on the overall benefits that credit cards would have for the organization.

But again, it was a risk to purchasing because the centralized credit card process actually reduced the different departments' flexibility when purchasing items. The other departments could have resented and resisted the process. The risk was that purchasing invested a great deal of time and effort into a process that could fail, and purchasing would lose credibility.

Summary

Purchasing influence increased in this organization. First, the process was centralized under a new purchasing director. Second, the new director was assertive and became involved in several areas within the organization in which purchasing previously had not been involved. The director took risks, but his political skills helped the process gain influence. Meanwhile, he made an effort to increase the purchasing employees' competencies.

CASE L: CONSUMER PRODUCTS

A multi-billion dollar consumer products corporation is the focus of this case study. It is a highly visible, multi-national corporation that has product recognition worldwide. The company consists of four major divisions, but the two largest divisions make up approximately 90 percent of the company's total revenues. These two divisions sell many different products that have a long tradition of brand recognition and loyalty. The two smaller divisions also have long traditions and high brand recognition but generally have smaller markets.

Because of the size of this corporation, the case focuses on only the primary division. This division accounts for nearly 50 percent of the company's total revenue and would be larger than many of its competitors. Another reason that the case focuses on only one division is that each division is managed autonomously.

The company generally produces its own products and markets them under its name. A review of the company's annual reports during the past 15 years indicated that it traditionally perceived itself as a marketing company. However, during the past five years it seemed to be emphasizing manufacturing and new product development much more. It could be said that the company now perceived itself equally as a marketing, product development, and production company.

Purchasing's Influence in Corporate Strategic Planning

This is an extremely large corporation, so it is only possible to relate to one of the divisions. In the case of this division, purchasing's influence was at an eight on a 10-point scale. The reason purchasing is allocated an eight is that it met some strenuous cost-saving goals, and the CEO used it as model. Even though this had traditionally been a market-driven company, a major letter from the chairman cited the importance of obtaining long-term relationships with suppliers in its effort to reduce costs and improve quality. Also, the purchasing directors from the various divisions were able to develop a supply integration team, and the CEO attended several of these meetings even though the task force was an informal entity. In addition, the CEO used several of the metrics developed by purchasing as a benchmark for corporate activity. The purchasing directors now had the "ear" of the CEO. This was a major change for purchasing within this organization.

Industrial Dynamics and Corporate Leadership

Approximately four years prior to this case analysis, the company retained an outside consulting group to benchmark the company's expenses compared to those of others in the industry. Apparently the board believed that the company's profit margins were not as great as they should be given its leadership in the various markets. The speculation was that the CEO was receiving extensive pressure from the board. At one point there was even speculation that the CEO might be asked to resign, but no public information surfaced.

The consultant's analysis indicated that the company's administrative and production expenses far exceeded competitors' expenses. The report was not well received and had little or no credibility among many top managers in the company. The manner in which the figures were developed was seriously questioned by many employees. A general feeling was that the CEO had used the consultants as a lightning rod to give attention to the cost structure.

But the outcome of the consulting report was a shocking directive from the CEO to all company employees making a major reduction in the cost structure. Many believed that the goals were unrealistic and the CEO was using them as a way to deflect attention from cost pressures in the entire industry...or maybe from his own performance. But the action brought much attention to the purchasing and materials function. Changes would have to be made in the purchasing process to meet the CEO's goals.

Corporate Structure

Each of the divisions was managed by a president who had rather independent financial responsibilities. The president was a member of the executive committee along with the corporate vice presidents of finance, legal affairs, governmental affairs, and corporate relations.

Each division had a corporate management structure and a plant management structure. Plant managers were generally responsible to a general manager at the production facility and had a loose dotted-line relationship to the corporate staff. Each division had a vice president of supply chain management. About a year ago this title replaced the previous one of vice president of operations.

The title change was a directive of the executive committee. In various divisions, different reorganizations occurred as a result of the title change. Each division had a director of purchasing reporting to the vice president of supply chain management. Also reporting to the vice president of supply chain management were the directors of manufacturing and logistics.

Each plant had a manager of purchasing. This manager reported to either the director of operations or the director of manufacturing within the plant. This individual had a dotted-line reporting relationship to the corporate purchasing director.

Purchasing Leadership

A new director of purchasing was named approximately two years ago. This individual had formerly been a director of manufacturing at a major plant and ultimately a general manager of a large production facility. He had no previous experience in purchasing. To quote this director, "I was surprised to be appointed as the purchasing director. Believe me, I have had more than my share of battles with the purchasing people. It seemed that I was always on their back."

In retrospect, he said this may be why he was named the director. He believed that there were many things that purchasing should be doing.

Purchasing Strategy

"Our goal is for the company to be noted for its supply strategy as well as its marketing strategy." This quote by the corporate purchasing director was a reference to the many case studies that had been written about the company's marketing strategies. The director believed that supply strategy was as important as marketing strategies in the 1990s; however, it was up to the purchasing group to convince the top executive group and the rest of the company of this fact. Furthermore, he believed that purchasing had a grand strategy that would make this point.

But the strategy had to be driven by cost savings. The purchasing function had a major goal to meet, so the strategy had to have immediate cost-savings goals.

The strategy had three legs to it. First, it was critical to have a strategy for each commodity group. Second, it was important to leverage buying across the entire corporation when appropriate for the commodity. The point was made that corrugated packaging and sugar were two commodities that were used throughout the corporation; however, each division purchased these commodities separately from each other. Accordingly, it was necessary to develop a grand strategy for the commodity.

A strategy could be cited for each commodity in the corporation. But the problem was that the director within one division had no relationship to directors in other divisions. Accordingly, the director in the largest division put together what he termed an Executive Supply Integration Team. This was an informal group made up of the directors with the purpose of determining how they could develop leverages through integrated buying. Even though the group was informal and had not been suggested by the CEO or anyone from the executive committee, the CEO visited several different task force meetings. He became extremely interested in what they were doing and asked for progress reports.

The third leg of the strategy was to reduce the supplier base and develop long-term alliances. The purchasing group believed that the best way to reduce costs and increase savings was by working closely with a few selected suppliers. But they also recognized that it was important to develop a new supplier strategy that was a major deviation from their traditional style. Rather than simply preparing RFBs and responding to them, it was necessary to work closely with suppliers.

These strategies were different from the famous approach taken by General Motors under Lopez. This company was a major player in the industry and could have possibly made some hard demands on its suppliers similar to the GM approach. But instead a much different strategy was chosen that emphasized supplier relationship development and it might be said that this approach was rather risky because it looked for long-term accomplishments rather than short-term goals. This strategy was pursued while the purchasing group was confronted with some demanding cost-savings goals.

Two other aspects were highly related to the strategy: hierarchical influence and metrics. The director within the largest division believed his greatest responsibility and challenge was to convince others throughout the organization that purchasing was a key to improving quality and savings. He spent much time trying to convince other functional areas about the importance of purchasing. One way he did this was through the use of various metrics. As one purchasing manager said, "The best way to let others know about the importance of purchasing is to let the numbers do the talking."

During the past two years many processes and outcomes had been monitored, and attempts had been made to measure them. It seemed that almost all of the managers believed that measurement was the way to evaluate their own performance and then let others know how they were doing.

A major focus of the measurement was to let the other groups know how purchasing could impact their cost structure. For instance, in one situation a long-term alliance resulted in a much higher quality ingredient. The purchasing department developed a metric to indicate to manufacturing how this would reduce their processing time while also reducing the reject rate.

The metrics were especially appreciated because they allowed purchasing to demonstrate how they could assist other groups in meeting their cost-savings goals. Additionally, the CEO used purchasing metrics as a model in several instances. The CEO apparently began to use the metrics for his own decision making.

Ultimately, purchasing exceeded its materials cost-saving goals while reducing administrative costs. Meanwhile, several other functional areas were having trouble meeting their goals. Purchasing was being used as a model for innovative cost-savings efforts.

Employee Competency

An integral part of the corporate strategy was the fact that the employees were generally well qualified for their jobs. Professional development was highly encouraged throughout the purchasing group. It was made clear that new skills would be required as the purchasing function changed perspectives from a traditional to a strategic approach. Concurrently, new, highly qualified employees with purchasing experience were hired whenever possible.

Summary

A major corporate-wide cost reduction program required that purchasing develop new strategies, but it also created an opportunity for purchasing. Concurrently, a new director of purchasing was hired with new ideas. Efforts to centralize buying, develop hierarchical influence, and encourage the use of metrics increased the function's influence. But the ultimate determinant for increased influence was that purchasing was able to exceed its cost-saving goals while other functions had difficulty meeting their goals.

CASE M: INFORMATION SERVICES

A multi-billion dollar information services corporation is the focus of this case. It has a large international presence and a major market share in its industry. In several markets, it dominates the competition, but the competition is always moving quickly. In fact, market share is difficult to determine because the products are changing so rapidly.

This entire industry has gone through a major realignment during the past five years. Although it is generally considered an information services corporation, many individuals would see it as a financial services corporation. Many mergers and acquisitions have occurred, and there has been a rapid pace of new product development.

Change and speed to market is currently driving this industry. Products are developing faster than at any time in history, so the entire company has to be able to adapt to change. This means that many managerial changes occur quickly, and reorganizations seem to be a common occurrence.

Purchasing's Influence in Corporate Strategic Planning

The relatively new vice president of purchasing has a highly visible position and a clear channel to the CEO even though he reports to another vice president. No formal executive planning committee exists, but the purchasing vice president is consulted on major issues on a regular basis. Purchasing has been successful at several high-risk endeavors that resulted in major cost savings. On different occasions in management newsletters and major presentations, the CEO has mentioned the importance of purchasing.

On the one-to-ten scale, purchasing influence is noted as a nine in this company. One reason for this rating is that the company does not purchase materials for its product. The product is services. However, capital equipment is essential for the delivery of services, and no capital can be acquired without the review of purchasing. Every indication is that purchasing has respect, credibility, and influence throughout the company and from the CEO.

Competition and Corporate Leadership

This is probably one of the most rapidly evolving industries in the world. Products delivered today were not even imagined five years ago. For certain segments of the company, competitors are a major force that did not exist a few years ago.

This company took a radical step approximately four years ago when it hired a former senior executive from a manufacturing firm to serve as CEO. This individual had no experience in the information services industry, but he had experience as a major consumer of information. But the important point is that his experience was in manufacturing.

As soon as he was appointed, the new CEO radically reorganized the company. Previously the company had been organized as a collection of small businesses with each business having its own staff. Few services were centralized, and most operating decisions were made independently within business units. No synergies were apparent between the business units. It was almost as if the corporation was a financial holding company.

With the reorganization, the company was aligned along product lines. Entire product lines were brought under different group presidents so that products would be better aligned with each other. Concurrently, the many service functions were brought together as corporate staff positions. This reorganization required massive movements of individuals, and many employees either voluntarily or involuntarily left the company during this period. Although it was a major change, it was done quickly.

Purchasing Organization

Although various activities were conducted at different locations around the world, the primary purchasing processes were centralized as much as possible during the reorganization. When appropriate, duplicate functions were eliminated.

Purchasing Leadership

Approximately one year after the reorganization began, a new vice president of purchasing was brought into the company. He had extensive purchasing experience in a related industry. This individual was a dynamic leader who quickly sent the message to all purchasing employees that purchasing was going to be a leader in the corporation.

He became well known for the statement, "Why should a person be doing something that can be done by a machine?" In other words, he was a major advocate of information systems. Any function that was considered routine was to be analyzed for possible computerization or elimination.

Another of his favorite statements was, "Strategic thinking and actions are how we create value. Routine activities do not create value." During an interview he stated, "I am a change agent who just happens to be involved in supply management."

Shortly before joining the company he completed the summer program at the Harvard Executive Development Institute. He said that the institute taught him the importance of thinking in terms of systems and processes rather than in terms of discrete actions. He believed that a major shortcoming of American management was that it was short-sighted and tended to think of everything in categories rather than as a larger system.

Purchasing Strategies

As mentioned, every effort was made to reduce routine activities. The word strategic was used in a similar vein as adding value. The question continually asked was, "How can purchasing add value to the corporation? "This question translated into initiatives. Top purchasing managers continually asked themselves and others what new initiatives they could implement that would add value.

One of the major initiatives was to look at possible outsourcing of services. Any service that the company provided either internally or externally was a possible target for outsourcing. The initial one was travel. At first, purchasing thought that it was a major accomplishment to become responsible for all corporate travel. However, as soon as the new vice president of purchasing joined the company, he asked a task force to look at the possibility of outsourcing all travel plans. This was accomplished within a year and set the stage. Purchasing became extensively involved in feasibility analyses for a number of different services, from the cafeteria to travel to computer maintenance.

The outsourcing was not completed with a bid process. Rather, the potential suppliers were asked to discuss the process with the purchaser. From a manufacturing perspective, it could be said that this was early supplier involvement. In one instance, a team of potential suppliers worked together to develop work specifications for the service that was to be outsourced.

The purchasing group made it clear that long-term alliances or partnerships were the desired goals. Accordingly, partnerships went along with the outsourcing and early supplier involvement.

Purchasing gained internal support for the outsourcing program because it had been successful. As one purchasing manager stated, "It is difficult to argue with success." With each initiative, measurable outcomes were established and results were published. The belief was that published information built in a commitment to results.

Between the success of new initiatives and the aggressive selling on the part of the top purchasing management, purchasing quickly became seen as valuable within the company. Many of the other line managers made comments about purchasing becoming the outsourcing division.

Employee Competence

The outsourcing success could not have been accomplished without highly qualified employees. One of the most senior directors as well as the vice president commented that the lack of good employees would be the greatest hindrance to the success of the purchasing group. They made it clear that they only wanted assertive purchasing professionals who had good human relations skills and appropriate analytical skills. Within one year, the company hired two recent MBA graduates who had both experience and education in purchasing management.

Summary

A major reorganization that resulted in centralized efforts, an assertive new vice president who created new purchasing initiatives, and success in outsourcing services provided an opportunity for purchasing to obtain influence within the company.

CASE N: ELECTRONIC MANUFACTURER

A multi-billion dollar company with a global presence in electronic devices, computer technology, and information systems is the focus of this case study. The company had quadrupled in size over the past 15 years. Plans are for the same or even greater growth during the next 15 years.

The company is often cited as a world-class organization that has been extremely innovative. Creativity has been fostered and rewarded throughout the corporation. It is generally considered a technological leader. Although it has failed at several endeavors, most of its technological ventures have been overwhelming successes. Also, in various surveys the company is frequently cited as having created an outstanding working environment.

Because the company has experienced such tremendous growth during the past decade, one of the fears among employees and outside observers is that it will become too large to manage.

Purchasing's Influence in Corporate Strategic Planning

An executive vice president is responsible for supply management strategy. The CEO and chairman have both given the supply management function highly visible support. The CEO has publicly stated that supply management is a major component of the company's future. On the one-to-ten scale, purchasing influence is rated at a nine or 10.

Industrial Dynamics

This is a rapidly developing industry. To quote the CEO, "We are seeing the greatest technological revolution in the history of the world. And we are at the heart of that revolution. Our challenge is to meet the demands associated with a pace of development heretofore unknown." This quote summarizes the industry's environment. In some ways the company attempted to develop new products for consumers who are not even aware of the needs yet. As the consumers became aware of the technological possibilities of new products, they became aware of the needs, but then other companies entered the same market. As a result, the company, and the entire industry, operated from a time-based strategy.

Because the technology is developing so rapidly, the global demand is difficult to predict. The company's supply and demand projections did not followed any predictable cycle during the past decade. This made capacity planning difficult throughout the industry. Shortages have occurred and sudden worldwide surpluses have developed.

Creativity was the foundation upon which the industry was established. Many stories existed of skunk works and think tanks. The prevailing attitude and culture was one of optimism and "If they can do it, we can too."

Corporate Leadership

The chairman was past the normal retirement age. Many considered him a giant of the industry if not a hero of American enterprise. Presidents of the United States have asked him for advice, and he has met with world leaders to discuss business issues. Even though he was not active in the daily activities of the corporation, his smallest suggestions held considerable weight.

Approximately two years ago he convened a three-day meeting of the corporation's top executives to review the company's planning parameters. Several top materials managers were present at that meeting. The primary outcome of the meeting was that capacity planning was a major issue that required attention. Shortly after the meeting, a new position was established: executive vice president of strategic supply management. This new position received the strong endorsement of everyone at the meeting.

Supply Management Leadership

The person who filled the new position was formerly the manager of a major manufacturing facility. Because this was a major facility, he had high visibility throughout the corporation and extensive experience. But he had no previous purchasing experience.

He believed that his major challenge was to develop both a planning model and strategic long-term relationships with key suppliers. He believed that the corporation was too big to develop some master plan that would fit the entire company and all supply needs. Rather, he wanted all of the supply managers to "think out-of-the-box" to develop some creative solutions. When asked what he meant by that, his reply was, "I don't know the solution. But I have enough confidence in our people to think that they will develop the answer."

This vice president didn't see himself as a decision maker or an implementer. Rather he believed that he was strictly a leader who was going to inspire the supply chain managers throughout the company to use their creativity to solve problems.

Purchasing Strategy

The supply chain concept was introduced into the company about one year ago and it already seemed to be strongly entrenched. Even though the concept had been used for only about a year, it was accompanied with major statements about the importance of supply to the future growth of the company. (Recall that the company was expected to double in size approximately every five years.) Each of the major divisions adopted the concept at the same time, so it was not a piecemeal adoption.

Accompanying the concept of supply chain was some organizational restructuring. Manufacturing and materials supply managers (formerly purchasing managers) were now at the same level and reported to supply managers. Operations directors were renamed supply chain managers.

The term buyer was essentially removed and replaced with the title of supplier management coordinator. The important point here is that the term relationship was in the new job description. The wording put an emphasis on long-term relationships and quality development rather than negotiations and price reduction. Quality and supplier development were a major theme of this position.

Efforts were being made to move supply chain down to the second- and third-tier suppliers. Although purchasing management did not feel this had been accomplished, involvement with second- and third-tier suppliers for each product class was the goal.

This company had been identified with participatory management for a number of years. Along with this, teams had been an integral part of the corporate culture for the past 15 years. This made cross-functional teams much easier to use.

For the past decade, purchasing had been involved in the early stages of product design. Also, purchasing had traditionally involved the suppliers at an early stage. Even though proprietary information had always been a challenge to manage, purchasing still believed it was necessary to involve suppliers.

Concurrent with such activities as early supplier involvement, long-term alliances and cross-functional teams, a strong push had been made to reduce routine activities. The company was one of the first to use purchasing cards corporate-wide. The concept of hiring a "buying agent" who responded to requisitions had been eliminated according to most managers. However, it was important that this concept did not reemerge, so purchasing management was always working to assure that the function remained proactive.

Proactive purchasing management was a term often used in the company. The exact meaning was not clear. One manager said that it meant, "To create, not simply not to respond." Another manager said that it meant, "Find ways to add value before someone else from a different department points it out to you." Still another person said that it meant, "Create solutions that make life easier for others in the business."

Corporate culture encouraged both proactive purchasing management and cross-functional teams. Purchasing was only consistent with the corporate culture when using these two approaches. In other words, the culture strongly supported purchasing's involvement in activities that would be extremely difficult to implement in other organizations.

Employee Competency

The company had grown so rapidly that many new employees had been assimilated into the purchasing process during the past decade. The traditional purchasing mentality in which the responsibility of purchasing was simply to execute POs had diminished. Many of the purchasing employees were engineers, which made it much easier for the group to receive credibility within the technical world and be involved early in the product design stage. Many of the others had business degrees with a strong background in value analysis, total cost of ownership, and so forth. The combination of backgrounds and education made purchasing a strong group that clearly added value to the supply chain.

Summary

Supply chain management had high visibility and made an impact in this company. The industry experienced rapid growth and supply was critical to the company's continued progress. The chairman and top executives recognized purchasing's importance. Accordingly, a highly visible senior executive was appointed to the key supply management position. Meanwhile, the corporate culture supported creative solutions to problems. This allowed the supply function to be creative and proactive. Top management expected supply management to make a significant contribution, and because it made a contribution, the supply function was included in corporate strategic planning.

CASE O: CONSUMER PRODUCTS

This corporation is a global manufacturer and marketer of consumer product goods. It has operations in more than 25 countries and markets more than 100 products in more than 125 countries with annual sales exceeding $10 billion. During the 1990s the company experienced steady growth in sales, profits, and stock values. The steady growth has been accomplished through increased product market share plus steady acquisitions of new products. The acquisitions have generally been accomplished in a friendly manner. The company has a reputation for providing a positive managerial environment for acquired firms. Another growth strategy is to acquire international businesses and to expand in areas with strong economies.

Purchasing's Influence in Corporate Strategic Planning

This case is different from any of the other cases in that it is primarily a corporation made up of many individual product lines that are run as independent profit centers. Although a single management philosophy theoretically permeates the company and it has one driving mission statement, it is still made up of many autonomous groups. In some of these units purchasing has extensive influence, while in others it may have limited influence.

For this case, purchasing is considered only within the context of the corporate staff. Within the executive staff, sourcing is seen as a driver in the low-cost or cost reduction corporate strategy. In published documents, sourcing is cited as a key component of the corporate strategy. The corporate purchasing director serves as a key liaison to the executive office. This individual is consulted on a regular basis. Largely based on documentation from the chairman's office and the frequency with which the chief purchasing officer has contact with the top executives, purchasing influence in this company is given a rating of seven on a 10-point scale.

Corporate Structure

"This is a corporation made up of 25 different companies. Some of the companies could have a major presence if independent while others are similar to the local grocery store." This quote from a manager on the corporate purchasing staff generally summarizes the corporate structure.

The corporate staff is relatively small. It consists of what may be considered internal consultants or support staff for the various functional areas as well as the corporate legal counsel, tax department, finance department,

and stockholder relations staff. The staff support groups such as marketing, manufacturing, and human resources have no direct line authority over the units within the company. However, they have a high level of expertise and have a direct channel to the CEO's office.

Purchasing Leadership

This case focuses on the corporate structure; therefore, the corporate director of purchasing in the corporate staff is discussed here. Remember that this individual had no formal authority over any of the purchasing managers in the business units. The purchasing director has an MBA from a leading university. He is a dynamic, analytical individual. It didn't take long to appreciate his leadership abilities.

In evaluating his own skills, the purchasing director said, "If I wasn't involved in purchasing, I would be trying to sell snow in Alaska." In other words, he was a tremendously dynamic leader who was always trying to sell his ideas. Because he had no direct authority over the business units, he knew it was a matter of "influence without authority."

He took the position less than two years before this case analysis. His predecessor was a retired military procurement officer who essentially managed MBE programs. Corporate leadership was obviously looking for a different type of person in this position. They went from a retired military officer to a quantitative-oriented MBA who was approximately 40 years old.

Within a year, the new director sold more than 10 of the purchasing managers throughout the corporation on the idea of establishing a purchasing council. This informal council compared practices and investigated opportunities for shared buying from centrally negotiated contracts. Suddenly, the business unit purchasing managers were asking the corporate director to become directly involved in their purchasing process. A corporate staff member had never become this directly involved.

Within two years, the corporate purchasing director had convinced the business units to support six corporate purchasing personnel. These individuals became support staff members on activities that could be leveraged across units. They also conducted research for the various units. The important point here is that the business units paid the salaries of these individuals. They were extremely well educated, highly analytical professionals.

The sourcing process gained visibility in the small corporate office, but more than visibility was gained... influence was obtained.

Purchasing Strategy

In addition to beginning to buy supplies that could be used across units, the corporate staff began to coordinate a benchmarking process. They did not conduct the actual benchmarking but they put together a procedure whereby the different units could benchmark. Within 20 months after the new director joined the company, the unit purchasing managers were meeting at least quarterly and the corporate staff coordinated the process.

As mentioned earlier, the purchasing director was highly quantitative. The benchmarking was a perfect match for his skills. In addition, he hired several individuals who had the aptitude for benchmarking various practices. But the benchmarking went beyond the normal comparison. It attempted to find ways that cost savings could be made and documented the type of savings that resulted. For instance, an entire analysis of the strategic use of EDI was made for the business units.

This benchmarking or quantitative analysis of cost-saving efforts allowed the purchasing managers at the business units to influence their business unit presidents. One of the business unit purchasing managers said, "Words can speak, but numbers convince." This is an important quote because the corporate purchasing director's influence was heard within the business unit. Measurement was definitely the influence agent in this corporation.

In addition to benchmarking and centralized contracts, the next corporate involvement was in the area of outsourcing. In this industry the business units were frequently chasing cheap labor due to the nature of the products. However, this became more difficult and gradually resulted in less of a competitive advantage. As a result, outsourcing of entire operations became more critical but required extremely thorough analysis. Purchasing became involved because the business units were essentially buying entire product lines and putting their brands on them.

The analytical expertise of the purchasing staff again became a factor. Corporate purchasing became known for its thorough analysis of outsourcing decisions. Within a short time, several employees who were hired in the corporate staff were relocated to one of the business units because of their expertise.

While the outsourcing analysis was occurring, the business unit heads were able to demonstrate some impressive numbers to the corporate executives. Major cost savings occurred with no loss in quality. Numbers were persuading.

But not all business units were involved with the outsourcing. Remember that the corporate purchasing staff was funded or paid for by the business units. Not all business units bought into the process. The corporate purchasing director strongly believed that "Those who pay for the game, play the game." Once the game began, he did not spend a lot of time trying to convince other business units to get involved. He strongly believed that the numbers would speak. Once the non-involved business units saw the results, they would buy into the process wherever possible.

Summary

Two themes dominated this case: leadership and metrics or analytical abilities. An extremely influential leader was able to develop a flurry of activity in a short period of time. His leadership style was a definite asset; however, he was able to accomplish the ultimate sell through the metrics. He firmly believed that numbers talked. This is how he obtained the attention of top managers, both in the business units and within the corporate structure.

Another interesting theme is that some of the business units bought into the quantitative analysis, and some did not. As the corporate director said, "Some of the purchasing groups are still clerical and will probably remain that way until forced out." In other words, some of the groups would have to be changed. He believed this would occur eventually through force from either the corporate executive group or from the unit presidents.

An important postscript to this case is that the corporate purchasing director left this company shortly after this case was written. He moved to another corporation that was approximately one-half the size of the case company, but it was still a large organization. He moved in as the number two supply management person where the process was much more centralized.

CASE P: COMPUTER-RELATED PRODUCTS

A leading producer of computer-related products is the focus of this case analysis. It has been an industrial leader in designing, producing, and marketing new products. Its general strategy has been to be the first to market with new products; however, in the past several years, its strategy has been to be a cost leader as well. This allows the company to maintain its market position even when its competitors are able to match them on the technology capabilities.

Because the company is a leader in an industry that has experienced tremendous growth, this company has been earning 20 percent revenue increases each year during the 1990s. To meet its capacity demands, the company has increased its production capacity throughout the world.

Purchasing's Influence in Corporate Strategic Planning

Purchasing may rate as high as a 10 on the 10-point scale for its level of influence in corporate planning. The primary reason for this is that the industry is experiencing tremendous worldwide growth, and purchasing is responsible for capital expenditures. The company cannot increase its capacity if purchasing cannot meet capital equipment needs. Accordingly, the vice president of purchasing is on the corporate planning committee and has extensive influence in its decisions. In addition, the chairman has made frequent references to the importance of purchasing and has directly consulted with purchasing for its advice on planning issues.

Industrial Dynamics

An extremely high barrier to entry is present in this industry, so a handful of giants dominate the competitive field. The competition was between a few U.S. and Japanese firms. Rapidly developing technology and continually increasing capacity demands were the name of the game in this industry. But the expenditures for increasing capacity became greater and greater. As a result, during the past several years, each new production facility exceeded the previous record in terms of size and capital investment. So each new facility and increased capacity represented a major risk. If worldwide demand were to weaken, impending disaster could have resulted. Although this industry represented an extremely sophisticated technology, competitors could not survive on technology alone. They had to be able to bring the technology to market at a breakneck pace so manufacturing was also a major facet of competitive strength.

Because the industry had been growing rapidly, suppliers also had trouble meeting demands. This meant that only a small number of suppliers were available,

particularly in the capital equipment area. Buyers were actually in competition to obtain commitments from the suppliers to provide them with the required equipment.

Corporate Leadership

The president of the company as well as the CEO were known to be dynamic, insightful leaders. They had received attention in the national press as being industrial leaders. Neither of these two individuals had formal experience in purchasing. However, approximately 10 years ago, the vice president responsible for technology development made a strong case for the importance of purchasing. The CEO supported the vice president's position at that time, and through the years the CEO gave strong support to the purchasing process.

Corporate Culture

"If you don't eat the dinosaurs, they will eat you. We don't ever want to look at another company and ask how they could do it but we couldn't." These two quotes or similar statements were frequently heard, and generally represented the corporate culture. The entire culture was one of a dynamic competitor that wanted to be number one. It definitely was not a place for individuals who wanted to rest on their achievements or who were interested in security. Innovation, hard work, and a high level of achievement were the norms throughout the company.

The same was true for purchasing. The standard way of doing things was never accepted as gospel. Because something worked in the past was no reason to make it sacred. Change was an accepted part of life. Just because things were going well was no reason to believe that things were good enough. This culture in purchasing allowed it to walk to the same beat as the remainder of the company and largely explains why the purchasing process was so proactive.

Corporate Strategy

This company was a market leader grounded in time-based strategies with a strong technological orientation. It wanted to remain a market leader, so it had to make tremendous capital investments in order to meet its capacity needs. This strategy was based on high risk, so it may be said that the entire corporation had a risk orientation. The fear was always present and articulated that if the company did not meet demand, customers would find replacements.

Purchasing Strategy and Structure

Purchasing definitely was not reactive in the traditional sense of the word. It was a leader of initiatives and had a wide span of responsibilities. Its most important responsibilities were probably in the areas of capital goods and facilities. These had become a multi-billion dollar expenditure in the 1990s. It also had responsibility for raw materials, MRO, and indirect purchases such as advertisements, promotion, and travel. Travel alone exceeded $100 million annually.

Purchasing activities were centralized under a vice president of purchasing who reported to a senior vice president of operations. Within the purchasing function, different groups were responsible for facilities and capital equipment, materials, components, international, MRO, and indirect purchases such as travel and advertising. But regardless of the area, certain strategies prevailed. Integral to the strategy for each area was a supplier relationship component. In fact, supplier relationships were a cornerstone of the sourcing strategy. The extent to which long-term alliances and supplier development would be part of the relationships was always considered. A total cost of ownership model was used to assure that price was not the only driving force when selecting suppliers. Part of the total cost model was a pay-for-performance feature. Rather than just looking at the front end of the contract, the longevity of the equipment and quality of the materials were evaluated. This ensured that the supplier concerns went beyond the sale and contract.

Supplier development was critical because of the pace at which the industry was moving. Suppliers had to be ready to meet the quality and technological demands required to remain competitive. Due to time-based strategies, early supplier involvement was also a standard feature of the purchasing strategy. Because of the supplier relationships, it had been standard practice to have the suppliers located within the various production facilities. The general philosophy was not to hide anything from suppliers. The suppliers wore the production company's badges and attended appropriate meetings. This allowed the suppliers to better understand the production process and make appropriate adjustments to their own equipment.

An extension of this philosophy is what may be termed "super suppliers." These suppliers had the buying company highly dependent upon them because they were the sole source for a crucial piece of capital equipment. In turn, the supplier was investing a great deal of time and money with the buyer and was possibly losing other sales opportunities as a result. A high degree of interdependence existed between the buyers and suppliers.

Meanwhile, when it came to indirect or MRO materials, a radically different strategy was used. All routine or clerical activities had been computerized whenever possible. EDI and purchase order cards had been successfully implemented. With these various activities, the purchasing process had been an integral part of the corporation's general strategy.

Also important was the use of teams. Teams were part of the company culture, so sourcing teams were a natural fit. Capital purchasing was organized around sourcing teams headed by purchasing personnel. This allowed the purchasing group to integrate its expertise with that of others in the organization on major decisions. Teams were also used on other major sourcing decisions in addition to the major capital expenditures.

Employee Competency and Leadership

These two concepts are highly related in this case. As a highly technical company, leadership was related to technical competency. Although most of the purchasing employees were educated as engineers, they had spent a great deal of time learning the technical aspects of the product. This allowed them to gain the credibility and respect of the technical employees. In turn, they were seen as leaders in the company.

The most visible purchasing managers almost had a zeal for their function. They were missionaries for the importance of purchasing. However, they seemed to believe that it was extremely important to let the numbers do the talking. In other words, they had the analytical tools to demonstrate the impact that material quality and cost could have on business operations. So they led by both reason and charisma.

The competence of the purchasing employees within the organization was generally high. Most of the employees had college degrees, and many had advanced degrees. In addition, many employees had professional certifications and were involved with professional development activities.

Summary

Purchasing in this company was highly influential because of the executive support, leadership, and the results that purchasing had produced. The purchasing process was able to support the overall corporate strategy so it was seen as influential. But what came first, the chicken or the egg? Purchasing had a highly professional and competent workforce. Top management allowed it to hire the best and brightest. In turn, this workforce was able to demonstrate that the support was warranted. Did the good workforce lead to the support or vice versa?

The industrial dynamics also led to purchasing's influence. The industry and company were developing at a phenomenal pace. This required major capital investments. Without good supplier relationships for the capital expenditures, the expansion would not have been possible. The company was able to deliver results and gained additional influence because of it.

The company culture also supported innovation. In turn, the innovation of the purchasing group produced results that indicated the function's importance. But the primary factor for its influence was probably that purchasing strategy reflected the overall corporate strategy. To implement the strategy, capital expenditures were important. Purchasing delivered in the same general way that the entire corporation delivered: innovation in a timely manner that kept it ahead of the competition.

CASE Q: HOSPITALITY

This case is distinctively different from the other cases because it involves two competitors from the hospitality industry. Both organizations are hotel networks. The hotel industry experienced rapid growth in the 1980s with numerous hotels being built. However, tax changes radically altered the advantage of building numerous rooms at individual facilities. As a result, the 1990s saw a retrenching or refocusing within the industry.

Because there was a limited advantage to building new facilities, cost containment within existing facilities or refocusing to meet customer needs were the trends. Major emphasis was placed on attempting to redirect a facility's niche market. Often this required a major refurbishing of a facility.

Both of these hotel networks had been actively involved in acquisitions of existing facilities during the past four to six years. But after that commonality, the two corporations started to deviate on their strategy. For ease of discussion, the two hotels will be referred to as Guesthouse and Traveleasy.

Purchasing's Influence in Corporate Strategic Decision Making

The case reveals that two competitors have dramatically different levels of influence due to purchasing leadership, organizational structure, and purchasing strategy. At Guesthouse the influence is rated as a seven on a one-to-ten scale. However, with Traveleasy influence is a three on a one-to-ten scale. Guesthouse has a vice president of corporate purchasing who reports directly to the president. Traveleasy also has a vice president of purchasing. The Guesthouse vice president is included in the planning committee, but the Traveleasy vice president has a small staff and is not a member of any top management committees. The Guesthouse corporate purchasing group has been adding responsibilities whereas the Traveleasy staff has been reduced and purchasing for many items has been outsourced. Guesthouse continues to add staff while Traveleasy is losing staff.

Corporate Structure

As is often the case in this industry, both corporations owned some facilities and managed others, and still others were operated as franchises under the corporate name. This case focuses on the facilities wholly owned by the corporations.

Within the corporate structure, many of the operations are conducted at the facility level because they differ radically from market to market and from facility to facility. Two hotels within the same city had a marked difference in orientation. Major differences also existed among cities and geographic regions of the United States as well as between a resort operation and a standard hotel with conference facilities. Consequently, some of the operations were conducted within a centralized corporate structure; however, even the marketing was often completed at the local level for major facilities.

Purchasing Structure

Both organizations maintained purchasing corporate staff as well as regional staff. The intent was for the corporate staff to support the regional staff. Guesthouse had eight regions within the Américas. Traveleasy had 15 regions plus two large independent facilities that essentially acted as a region.

But here is where the two competitors differed. Guesthouse had been building its corporate function while Traveleasy had been decentralizing. In the decentralization, Traveleasy had been outsourcing part of the purchasing process. Traveleasy had contracted with a purchasing services firm to support the purchase of many of its services and commodities. For instance, Traveleasy outsourced its purchases of operational items within the rooms such as soaps, linens, beds, and other furniture. Guesthouse, however performed all of these services at the corporate level.

Here a similarity exists between the two organizations. At both companies, any of the regional departments could either use the corporate-arranged purchases or they could conduct their own purchasing for an item. The regional purchasing managers for Guesthouse and Traveleasy were not required to use corporate services.

A direct comparison between the size of purchases run through corporate services for the two companies was not possible because of size differences and lack of information disclosure. However, it became obvious that many more activities were conducted through Guesthouse corporate offices than through the purchasing services contracted by Traveleasy. The most observable measure of purchasing activity was that Guesthouse corporate purchasing was adding staff to meet the needs of its regional customers and it was moving into nontraditional areas. Meanwhile, for Traveleasy the regional offices were taking over more of the purchases rather than using the outsourcing firm. The purchasing services firm for Traveleasy was slightly decreasing.

Guesthouse's centralized purchasing function had much greater visibility within the corporate structure. This visibility may have been one reason that it was influential in corporate strategic planning. But the overall strategy was also a factor.

Purchasing Strategy

Traveleasy purchasing was a traditional transaction process. This company essentially viewed its function as one of meeting internal customer needs. It did not believe the function was to help understand or define the needs. Meanwhile, Guesthouse believed that the purchasing function was to find ways to reduce overall costs and add value to the organization.

An example that demonstrated the difference between the two purchasing processes was that Guesthouse developed a strategy to outsource engineering at many of their locations. This is a high-risk endeavor because engineering is so crucial to quality service. Even though it is a risky endeavor, purchasing organized a cross-functional team that analyzed alternatives and made a recommendation to the executive planning group. One of the recommendations was that outsourcing would be feasible at certain facilities but not at others.

Meanwhile, at Traveleasy the purchasing group was trying to encourage the engineering group to purchase from corporate contracts. The engineering group frequently bypassed purchasing for certain items even though purchasing had a blanket contract with a supplier.

Another example demonstrated the difference between the two organizations in purchasing strategy. Guesthouse developed a long-term contract with a producer of soaps and similar items with the Guesthouse corporate name on them. However, the logo had to change from one facility to another in order to identify the facility's specific location. In this way, the corporate contract could provide cost savings for the regions. Meanwhile, no adaptation for the regions was done with Traveleasy.

To use a common phrase, Guesthouse had a proactive purchasing strategy while Traveleasy had a purchasing transaction approach. Many of Traveleasy's transactions were simply outsourced.

Purchasing Leadership

Why were the two organizations conducting such dissimilar purchasing strategies? A leading cause seemed to be the leadership within the two companies. At Traveleasy, the vice president of purchasing was formerly a facility operations manager who admitted he preferred the more relaxed pace in purchasing. His salary was about the same in purchasing as it had been in facility management. So why put up with the "rat race" in operations? He believed his major purpose was to work with the purchasing services firm to ensure that it served the company well.

The vice president of purchasing for Guesthouse had extensive purchasing management experience in the hospitality industry. He had begun at smaller facilities and gradually worked his way to the vice presidency. He was a zealous believer in the value that purchasing could add to the organization. He believed in developing models that could show the value that purchasing was adding. He said, "I am continually looking for ways that I can best use the people in the department to ensure that we are serving the entire corporation." He went on to say that he loved "to try to show up marketing" to demonstrate the importance of purchasing. Within six years as vice president, he had definitely influenced people. To support this point, he said that over half of his job was direct sales. He sold the executive group (of which he was a member), he sold his employees, and he sold all of the facilities managers on the importance of purchasing.

The Guesthouse vice president used measurements to sell purchasing's value. He was continually trying to develop creative metrics and benchmarks that could be used to evaluate purchasing performance. But he also used the measures to show other departments the value that purchasing could add.

Summary

This case is different from the other cases in that direct comparisons are made between two hospitality companies. The two companies are dramatically different in their purchasing structure. One is centralized, and the other is decentralized and has outsourced much of its purchasing process. The two organizations have dissimilar purchasing strategies. One is proactive, while the other is reactive or even routine. Finally, the two vice presidents are 180 degrees apart in their beliefs about their function and role.

But a question remains. What effect did the CEOs of the two companies have on these differences? The answer necessitates a return to the basic question, "Did the two CEOs have different expectations that created the differences?" The differences were so dramatic that it was difficult to determine the role of the CEOs in relationship to purchasing. However, Guesthouse purchasing seemed to change dramatically after the present vice president was retained. An interesting point, however, is that the vice president was brought in from the outside, and major changes occurred after that. It is possible that the Guesthouse CEO saw the need for proactive purchasing. It was not possible to interview the CEO at either Guesthouse or Traveleasy, so further information was not obtained.

CASE R: HEALTHCARE

Rather than looking at one organization, this case concerns a type of organization: mid-sized hospitals. A short background indicates why hospitals were analyzed. The initial intent was to have a hospital as a case study because it would represent organizational structure and industry different from the other cases. Consequently, three different hospital systems were studied.

Purchasing's Influence in Corporate Strategic Planning

For each of these three hospitals, purchasing influence was as low or lower than at any of the other organizations studied. Nobody in purchasing had a high-visibility position. In each hospital, the manager of purchasing reported to a director-level position either in finance or in materials. Purchasing salaries at these hospitals were comparable to purchasing salaries in other industries. However, purchasing was not consulted on major hospital decisions. In addition, the purchasing departments had small staffs and did not enjoy any of the status symbols such as office space possessed by other functional areas within the hospital. On the one-to-ten scale, the hospital purchasing departments' influence was rated at a three.

Hospital Environment

Hospitals are in a unique environment. Theoretically, they are not supposed to compete with one another. However, they market themselves as being better than the others. This means that their real competition is against a benchmark or standard of quality rather than other hospitals. Another irony is that all three hospital systems involved with this study were not-for-profit organizations; however, they have to be efficient and effective in order to remain in existence. So according to governmental regulations they are non-competitive organizations that compete against standards. In the healthcare environment of the 1990s, they must control costs.

Another way that hospitals are different from other organizations is that they provide a special product: healthcare. Consumers will tend to complain about costs and service in this industry, but they do not have the freedom to abstain from purchasing the product. An example demonstrates the point. A consumer may want a new car, but interest may subside when costs and benefits are analyzed. Subsequently, the consumer stops shopping for a new vehicle and continues driving the old product. The car manufacturer has an incentive to hold down costs and improve the product.

But when a person needs a gall bladder operation, the consumer does not shop for alternatives. No doubt exists that the person will have the operation. Suddenly, quality is taken for granted, and price lacks relevance. The consumer is only interested in obtaining the required health services.

How does this relate to purchasing? The top hospital administrators maintain that costs are important, but will they refuse to buy the latest equipment if it exceeds budgets? Probably not. If the product helps deliver health services, it will be purchased. So the primary objective is to have whatever is required to deliver the best product and keep the consumer satisfied. In a time of healthcare needs, costs suddenly become a minor issue. Most consumers know the relative price of a Mercedes Benz compared to a Ford, but they do not know the price of an ultra-sound compared to an MRI.

Purchasing probably cannot conduct a cost-benefit analysis of the capital equipment needs for the two procedures and expect to influence management decisions. However, purchasing will be asked to attempt to save money on rubber gloves while the hospital spends $1.25 million on an MRI that is not fully utilized.

The supplier of the MRI has little reason to be price competitive. The MRI is such a specialized piece of equipment that few competitors exist.

Still another reason exists that hospitals operate in a unique environment. Dual management control exists. This means that the hospital administrators may control certain aspects of the organization; however, the medical doctors have control over other domains, even if the policy and procedures state that management controls them. The medical doctors technically are not even hospital employees. They simply have the privilege of practicing within the hospital.

An example demonstrates this point. A surgeon may be performing a hip replacement. The purchasing department has developed a contract with a major supplier of artificial hips at $990 per unit. However, the medical doctor (M.D.) states that in order to perform the procedures at maximum efficiency, a hip costing $1500 is necessary. Technically, little difference may exist between the two products, and the hospital would save $500 purchasing from the contracted company. Still, in many situations, the M.D. will prevail, and the $1500 hip will be used. The purchasing department has little influence in this situation because the M.D. controls the purchase request.

Capitation may change all of this, or so it would seem. With capitation the hospital provides healthcare for a number of individuals at a set rate per year. For instance, a hospital may contract to provide all health services for a school system at $1000 per employee per year. If an employee requires no health services, the hospital financially benefits; but if a school system employee requires major services, it could be to the hospital's financial disadvantage.

In this situation, cost containment becomes a major concern. Now if an employee needs a hip replacement, the purchasing department has every reason to pressure the M.D. to use the hip unit for which the hospital has a contract. It seems that purchasing would obtain additional influence with capitation.

But to what extent can purchasing pressure the M.D. to use the unit for which purchasing has a contract? This would depend upon the top administrators' support.

Congruence with Organizational Mission

Healthcare professionals dominate healthcare organizations. Although this is not a profound statement, it is important to consider. People with business degrees tend to dominate the purchasing profession within healthcare organizations. In other words, purchasing professionals conducting business analysis are managing the purchasing process while healthcare professionals manage most other aspects of the organization. The personal perspectives and missions differ from one another of these two groups of professionals.

The purchasing professional presents arguments for cost reductions and value analysis of capital equipment; but, top management holds primary interest in quality of healthcare. Quality is not always related to cost. Although top managers say they are interested in cost containment, and the health industry maintains it is cost conscious, quality of healthcare remains the number one goal regardless of cost. In the healthcare industry, traditional purchasing is often at odds with the corporate mission.

Each of the three hospitals provided an example of a major capital equipment purchase. In each case, the final purchase was authorized by a capital equipment team. The only aspect that was seriously considered in each purchase was the number of features provided by the equipment. Although, in each case, the warranty was considered, total cost was not a major factor, and no formal cost models were used. The average cost for each piece of equipment was near $1 million.

In each of these examples, the healthcare providers were making the major decisions. Purchasing was responsible for contracting.

Purchasing Strategy

In each of the three hospitals, purchasing was making a major attempt to move away from the transaction mode to a contractual mode. Efficiencies in the administrative processes were pursued, especially through such activities as EDI, reducing the supplier base and working with group purchasing initiatives. Purchasing was also involved in capital equipment teams as well as other important cross-functional teams.

Outsourcing also was being reviewed within each hospital. Food services, laundry services, and even engineering were being investigated for potential outsourcing. In general, it could be said that each of the hospitals was pursuing a proactive purchasing strategy.

Employee Competency

In each of the hospitals, purchasing employees had a high level of professionalism. Each hospital had a least one individual with a C.P.M. designation and another with an advanced degree in business. Professional development activities were encouraged, and a high percentage of employees held memberships in professional organizations.

Summary

Qualified employees and proactive purchasing strategies did not translate to high levels of influence within these organizations. The nature of the organization and its mission is generally not consistent with the purchasing process. A strong statement can be made about the impact that the industry and organization has on purchasing's influence within the organization.

Can it be said that regardless of what purchasing does it will always have little influence in corporate strategic planning within hospitals? The safe answer seems to be yes. However, this is not to say that purchasing will not have an impact on cost savings within the hospital. Also, healthcare may be a reasonably good career track for purchasing professionals as their salaries for a mid-management position are competitive with manufacturing. However, it is highly doubtful that in the near future we will see many a vice presidents of purchasing within hospitals.

CASE S: ELECTRICAL UTILITY

A mid-sized electrical utility in an eastern metropolitan area is the focus of this study. This public utility had the same concerns as most utilities throughout the United States. First, it was under the control of a public utility commission; second, the impending issues of competition had to be addressed; and third, attempts had to be made to reduce variable costs. An additional concern for this utility was that its market was expanding, so it had to develop greater capacity or face new competition. At the same time, the rate commission had restricted the company's rate increases, which made it difficult to generate capital for potential expansion.

Purchasing's Influence in Corporate Strategic Planning

Purchasing's influence changed dramatically over two to three years. During this time, a new vice president of purchasing was named. This individual reported directly to the third most influential person in the corporation. The purchasing process was renamed supply chain management, and many managers were assigned to the new vice president. The vice president was assigned to the executive planning committee within a year of his hire date. On the one-to-ten scale, supply management influence was nine.

Financial Performance

As was the case with many utilities, this company's financial performance was relatively poor in the late 1980s. The stock price was depressed, and the dividends, ever so important with public utilities, were slipping. As a result of these lower dividends, the company had to deal with negative press. However, most startling of all was the fact that a much larger public utility made an effort to purchase the company. This was the first time that the executive managers had ever faced such an outside threat, and they were not prepared for it.

The takeover effort was repealed by the company's board, and the effort did not become hostile; however, the executive group was uneasy for nearly six months. One of the main reasons they were uneasy is that much of the business press shed negative light on the company.

The negative press in combination with the poor financial performance and the abated takeover effort set the executive group in action. A consulting firm was asked to make a major review of the company's strategy and operations. Within the context of this case, no new top executives were named, but it was obvious that external pressures were the cause of some major changes. As the case developed, it became obvious these "outside" pressures were a major factor in helping to create more influence for purchasing.

Corporate Strategy

As a result of the consultant's review, two major conditions were revealed that were particularly relevant to purchasing/materials management: impending competition from other sources of electrical power and reduction of variable costs. For four straight years the chairman emphasized these concepts in his annual report.

The consultant determined that this utility had one of the highest employee-customer ratios in the industry. This naturally resulted in extremely high administrative costs. One of the reasons for the high costs was that information systems were not being used effectively. Executive management established a plan to reduce costs through a reduction of administrative costs by better using information systems.

Purchasing Leadership

In an effort to reduce costs, a vice president of purchasing was hired. Three important points emerged about this new person. First, this was the first time the company had a purchasing vice presidential position. Second, the person was hired from the outside. Apparently no serious consideration was given to hiring an inside manager. Third, the applicants were interviewed by the entire executive committee.

These three points demonstrate the importance of this new position. It gave the new vice president extensive influence prior to joining the company.

The person hired for the new position had vast experience with a Fortune 100 company that possessed a reputation for advanced management practices. He believed that the reason he was given the job was that during the interview he made a strong argument for adapting the supply chain concept and centralizing various activities under his leadership. The executive group agreed with this proposal prior to hiring him.

The vice president reported to the chief operating officer, who was the third most influential person in the entire corporation (after the chairman and the CEO). The vice president of purchasing was at the same level as the chief financial officer and the other major functional heads.

The new vice president began with the company two years prior to this case. The following section of this discussion indicates that he was able to build coalitions with other top managers and gain tremendous support from his supply management employees.

Proactive Purchasing Strategy

The executive committee directed every administrative function to analyze its use of information systems. An *ad hoc* committee for information systems was established in which a senior manager of purchasing was involved. This occurred immediately after the new vice president joined the company.

The vice president and a purchasing manager took an initiative with the committee by suggesting that the supply process be entirely reengineered. This was important for two reasons: (1) the entire management group was looking at the *ad hoc* committee to see what would occur, and (2) supply management grabbed much of the attention. The committee supported all of the supply management reengineering efforts, and positive results were quickly recognized.

The supply management group demonstrated how cost savings could be achieved by implementing a credit card system and computerizing the purchasing process as much as possible. A more important effect on purchasing influence was that the inventory and logistics systems were centralized under the supply chain vice president. Little resistance to the change was exercised by the other managers because the tacit influence of the *ad hoc* committee was ever present.

The combination of implementing information systems and centralization of supply activities was particularly important in this case. It demonstrated that supply management could make a major impact on variable costs, and centralization made the entire function much more visible.

The timing was perfect for the new vice president, but he also was a masterful leader. During an interview, he never took any credit for the dramatic changes, and he never sounded as if he had any great insights. It appeared that he could be a master at convincing everyone that they could make a major contribution to the organization. This impression was confirmed by various supply managers. Not one negative word was uttered about the vice president. He appeared to be an able coalition builder.

Employee Competence

As the reorganization took place, many employees formerly in purchasing lost influence. Those employees who maintained the mental set that purchasing's function was to receive and fill POs either were reengineered out of a job or pursued dramatic re-training. Within two years, 60 percent of the former purchasing positions were eliminated.

Many of the employees assigned to supply management did not seem to perceive themselves as purchasing professionals. They were engineers who were in supply management. This brought some new insights to the process; however, it also was necessary to educate/train these individuals on the basic procurement processes. This was accomplished by requiring everyone to receive a certain amount of external training on purchasing management within 18 months of being assigned to supply management.

Summary

An outside event stimulated top management to respond. As a result, management identified inordinately high variable costs. One of the corrective actions to reduce these costs was to hire a vice president of supply chain management. They selected a powerful leader who was able to build coalitions and create a high level of influence for purchasing. The strategies he led further increased the perceived impact of purchasing. The increased influence was initially stimulated by an outside event and enhanced through strong purchasing leadership and a proactive strategy.

CASE T: MANUFACTURING COMPANY

This case analyzes a design and manufacturing company with annual sales of approximately $500 million. It had a unique market niche but existed with the continual fear that a much larger organization could enter its market. Top management believed that two strategies existed for protecting itself against competitors. First, the company followed a philosophy of continual improvement to improve its products' quality and to develop operating efficiencies. Second, its goal was to further expand its already dominant share of the niche market. To accomplish this second goal, it was necessary to expand the company's production capacity.

During the past five years the company had experienced record sales and profits. More importantly, it had increased its market share within the niche market. These two events allowed the company to reinvest more of its revenue into additional production capacity as well as research and development.

Purchasing's Influence in Corporate Strategic Planning

It was difficult to determine the extent of purchasing's influence. But no doubt its influence increased as a result of recent events. The new title of supply management vice president was important for purchasing influence, and more executive discussion involved purchasing issues. However, the full impact of many recent changes had not been determined at the time of this case study. On the one-to-ten rating scale, purchasing influence was rated a seven. But due to the many recent changes, it was difficult to conclude firmly what the extent of purchasing influence would be over time.

Competition

The event most feared by management eventually became a reality. A major corporation that had already invested in comparable basic manufacturing capabilities announced that it was going to enter this market. Concurrently, the company's board of directors believed that net profits had not been acceptable over the past three years. This presented a dilemma because profits had been above average for the industry, but much capital reinvestment was required for expansion. Consequently, dividends were not as high as those at comparable companies. The board apparently was looking for immediate income rather than long-term growth. But to make matters worse, a new competitor entered the market.

Corporate Leadership

The board unceremoniously asked the president to resign, and a new president was quickly named. The new president was young for his position — approximately 45 years old — and had been employed by a much larger company that was a customer of this case company. The young president moved quickly. He immediately retained a consulting firm to analyze the company's strategy and production structure. Within six months the company had a new logo and launched a promotional program describing the "new" company.

An important point is that the new president had spent most of his career in marketing. His former company was generally considered a creative marketing organization. When he took over his new position, he brought an assistant with him who had a manufacturing background. This assistant had experience in manufacturing, industrial engineering, and purchasing.

Supply Chain Management

At about the same time that the president introduced the new logo and stated that the entire company would be "new," he announced a major reorganization. The biggest change was that the former operational vice president was reassigned as the vice president of supply chain. This vice president reported directly to the president/CEO. The reorganization announcement stated, "...the supply chain is crucial to our company's success. The vice president of supply chain will be responsible for some of the most important processes in our company." Transportation, purchasing, manufacturing, and distribution all reported to the vice president of supply chain.

The reorganization was a dramatic enhancement for purchasing. Formerly the manager of purchasing reported to the director of manufacturing. Now the purchasing position was elevated to a high organizational level and reported to the vice president. Purchasing was now at the same level as other comparable functions; the entire supply process gained increased importance within the organizational chart.

At this point it can be said that an outside force, a new CEO, gave the purchasing process additional influence within the strategic aspects of the company.

Purchasing Leadership

Much of the increase in influence may be attributed to events external to the purchasing group. However, the former manager who was promoted to the new position — director of purchasing — had already set some positive initiatives in place. It can be speculated that the assistant to the CEO who entered the company six months before the change was pleased with what he saw. Also, the new vice president of supply chain had to be impressed.

The purchasing director has already been influential in developing commodity teams and implementing a credit card system. He apparently accomplished this with little support from the director of manufacturing to whom he formerly reported. In fact, the purchasing director stated, "My former boss did not bother me much one way or the other. I don't believe he was too interested in purchasing, but he did not get in my way. But the vice president of supply chain provided much more support to the purchasing director, so it was much easier to accomplish my initiatives."

The important point here is that upper management apparently did not establish many goals for the purchasing group. It was purchasing's responsibility to set its own initiatives, but then upper management would support them. The initiatives had to be established within purchasing.

It may be said that purchasing's increased influence consisted of an interaction between additional organizational support for purchasing and leadership from the purchasing group.

Purchasing Strategy

Immediately after the new structure was implemented, the purchasing director made a strategic decision. He asked the vice president of supply chain to include purchasing on all new product teams. He presented an extremely elaborate proposal for justifying his request. A major part of the proposal was a plan for developing formal supplier partnerships. He believed that early involvement would lead to product improvement and cost reductions.

The result was that the vice president asked the purchasing director to complete a thorough analysis of the company's supplier relationships. Within two months the purchasing group had developed and recommended a thorough procedure for managing suppliers. Two important aspects of the policy were: (1) back-door selling would be highly discouraged and (2) all major purchases, regardless of the department or function, would have to be reviewed by the purchasing department. A cost-savings-and-quality-improvement rationale was presented; however, it was also a major step toward purchasing's involvement in direct or non-traditional purchases.

The recommended policy was thoroughly discussed by the major parties in the supply chain group. However, most parties agreed that it generally met with approval as everyone perceived it as an attempt to improve the supply management process.

At the time of this case analysis, the policy had *de facto* acceptance within the firm but had not been implemented. While the recommended policy was being reviewed, the purchasing group also was developing a company policy for formalizing partnerships. This policy or procedure would also have to be reviewed and accepted by the supply chain group.

These various activities were making the entire supply chain management group much more aware of the purchasing process. At the same time, the vice president said that he found himself frequently addressing purchasing issues in the executive committee meetings.

Employee Competency

At this point, it appears that increased influence was the result of external issues, purchasing leadership, and purchasing strategies. However, the abilities as well as the assertive and creative nature of the purchasing employees also appeared to be a contributing factor. More than 80 percent of the purchasing group employees were either actively pursing their C.P.M. certifications or had already achieved them. A sense of excitement about the purchasing profession could be detected when visiting with these employees. They believed that purchasing was vital to the success of the firm, and they wanted everyone else to believe it.

Was this excitement a result of the purchasing director's leadership? He had hired good people who shared his excitement. No doubt the purchasing department consisted of a highly professional group of employees who were trying to implement leading-edge ideas.

Summary

External events, in combination with strong leadership and a proactive purchasing strategy, increased purchasing's influence. It is difficult to determine if a specific cause-and-effect relationship could be established, however. The leadership would not have had such a strong impact if it were not for the external events. At the same time, strong leadership with a proactive strategy was required to maximize the impact of the external events. No doubt the influence of purchasing dramatically increased with the combination of events.

CASE U: ELECTRONICS MANUFACTURER

This case investigates purchasing at a $5 billion manufacturer of electronic devices. The company employed approximately 45,000 people and conducted business in nearly 100 countries; however, close to two-thirds of its sales were in the United States. The company consisted of three divisions that each accounted for about one-third of the company's revenues. During the 1990s, the company had experienced approximately a five-percent revenue increase each year; however, earnings had not increased accordingly and actually decreased in two recent years.

Purchasing's Influence in Corporate Strategic Planning

The corporate vice president of purchasing was on the corporate planning committee. Also, each of the divisional vice presidents were on the divisional planning committees. New product development was a major facet of the corporate strategic plan, and purchasing was integrally involved in the process. In addition, time-to-market was an essential aspect of the company strategy, and again purchasing's strategy focused on time-based considerations. No doubt purchasing was an integral part of the corporate strategy.

Other symptoms of purchasing's influence were the authorization it received to hire highly competent professionals. In addition, each of the divisions allocated purchasing a training and development budget that was probably slightly larger than the budget for some of the other functions. On the one-to-ten scale, purchasing's influence was rated a nine.

Corporate Strategy

During the previous several years, sales increased but earnings remained flat or decreased. For approximately five years, the chairman mentioned the importance of reducing costs; however, it was not until two years ago that a definite cost reduction target was established. The chairman stated that within two years, it would be mandatory to "operate more efficiently than ever." Accordingly, official documents stated that it was necessary to reduce outside purchases by $275 million. While reducing outside costs, it would be necessary to improve speed to market and broaden the product mix. And, at the same time, the company's hope was to increase sales by becoming more aggressive in global markets.

Purchasing Organizational Structure

Shortly after the chairman announced the target to reduce outside purchases, he named a new corporate vice president of supply management. This person was hired from outside the company. Prior to joining the company, he had more than 20 years of experience in a variety of functions including marketing analysis and production, but only about two years in purchasing. His strength was probably his variety of experiences within the industry. When asked what he considered to be his outstanding strength, he stated, "I have been in the industry a long time and know what makes it work. However, procurement's value has never really been appreciated, but now the top people are beginning to see its value. What I brought was a new way of looking at things."

The new corporate vice president immediately announced that a new position of vice president would be created in each of the three divisions. Within two of the divisions a director was promoted to fill the new vice presidential slots while in the third division a person was hired from the outside. The corporate vice president provided a support function for the three divisional vice presidents. He had a small staff of professionals skilled in financial and quantitative analysis. The corporate vice president also sat on the executive planning committee. Meanwhile, the three divisional vice presidents were on the divisional planning committees.

The purchasing function within each of the divisions was centralized prior to the new positions being established. However, it was made clear with the new vice president positions that the supply function would be at the same level of importance as the other functional areas.

The new positions, along with the increasing materials expenses, gave the function a new sense of clout. This was clearly indicated with the new hiring that took place within the function. Because of the flat earnings and increasing administrative expenses, little new hiring occurred elsewhere in the company. However, supply management was authorized to hire several highly-qualified and well-paid professionals.

Purchasing Strategy

A major component of the corporate strategy was to develop a broader product mix and get the products to market quickly. Consistent with this strategy, purchasing was involved in the new product design and included suppliers in the process early. Purchasing attempted to develop some creative alliances with suppliers. Under these agreements, suppliers would share in risks and returns. This was a relatively new concept for the company, so some creative approaches were required. Purchasing's main goal was to reduce the supply base and become much more involved with the suppliers.

Much emphasis was placed on co-location of suppliers during the product development and initial production stages. Co-location had been practiced during the production process but not during the early stages of design and prototype production.

The interesting point here is that the company was having trouble controlling its costs; however, the purchasing staff did not seem to focus strictly on price. The corporate vice president made a strong argument for controlling costs through long-term contracts and early involvement of suppliers. To quote the vice president, "The key to the relationship is the contract. Price is an outcome of the relationship. If you have a good understanding of each other's needs, the price will be right."

Consistent with the corporate vice president's philosophy, each division developed a strategy for commodity groups. More than six months was taken by purchasing to develop these strategies and articulate them to the executive planning committee. Within the strategies was an elaborate statement about the type of supplier relationships that would best fit different commodities.

Another purchasing strategy was to get much more involved in value analysis and measurement of costs. The corporate vice president and the divisional vice presidents hired individuals who had engineering or financial analysis backgrounds. These professionals brought an analytical dimension to purchasing that it did not formerly possess.

Because of its new analytical ability, purchasing was asked to become involved in the make-versus-buy decisions. Five years prior to this case analysis, the majority of these decisions would have been made by a specialized product planning group. This group primarily consisted of engineers. As purchasing was increasing in size and influence, the product planning groups were shrinking.

In addition to assuming responsibility for the make-versus-buy decision, purchasing also became more and more involved in the outsourcing process. This was related to purchasing's involvement with suppliers in the early design stages of the product development.

Purchasing Leadership and Employee Competence

The top purchasing executives seemed to lead through results. In other words, they continuously attempted to demonstrate the results of their strategies with the belief that this would result in greater support for supply management. Their efforts seemed to obtain results.

Purchasing leadership appeared to have success when it asked for additional resources and employees. This group also asked for more responsibility in such areas as product design and related activities. In order to handle this additional responsibility, the purchasing leadership obtained management's approval to hire sophisticated employees who had advanced degrees. In addition, current employees were approved for extensive advanced education and training.

Because purchasing was able to develop measures and demonstrate results, purchasing experienced a positive reception. Employees were allowed to take risks — and they did.

When a divisional vice president was asked about the type of employees he liked, he quickly responded, "We need the three A's: analytical, articulate, and aggressive." He elaborated by saying that the employees had to be able to exert influence up and down the hierarchy. They had to be analytical in order to solve problems and measure their results. They were asked to work on teams, so they had to be team players who could listen but also sell others on the importance of purchasing. They had to be aggressive in order to find and solve new problems. This is how they added value. They didn't wait for the problems to come to them.

The theme that was frequently mentioned by purchasing employees was, "Add value, add function, reduce costs." The interesting aspect of this was that the emphasis on purchasing initially seemed to come out of the need to reduce material expenses; however, it was obvious that purchasing leadership, through the efforts of competent employees, had been able to move the function beyond one of simply reducing costs.

Summary

Revenues had grown, but material expenses seemed to grow more quickly than revenues. As a result, emphasis was placed on purchasing activities being conducted by individuals in new vice presidential positions. In addition, a number of highly-qualified employees were hired. These new employees were able to demonstrate purchasing's added value which, in turn, resulted in even more influence for the function.

APPENDIX B: INITIAL MODEL AND EXPLANATION •

EXECUTIVE SUMMARY

This research question was addressed for the Center for Advanced Purchasing Studies: *What conditions create influence for the purchasing function in corporate strategic planning?* The model presented in Figure 3 was developed as the result of a thorough review of the research literature, discussions with academic researchers and purchasing executives, and an in-depth analysis of 21 in-depth case studies of 24 organizations. Following is a brief description of this model.

Each of the boxes represent a condition that affects the influence that purchasing has in corporate strategic planning. The diagram is presented in a linear fashion; however, each condition affects all other conditions shown.

The first two conditions in the model are also the most important: industrial dynamics and executive leadership. Industrial dynamics is the general economic condition of the industry and the extent to which purchasing is vital within that industry. The finding is that when an industry is facing severe competition or experiences a major economic downturn, purchasing becomes more important. Executive leadership is the CEO or comparable executive who must believe in the importance of purchasing and provide support for the function. Both of these conditions are generally considered external conditions. Each condition is essentially outside the control of purchasing and may have either a positive or negative impact on purchasing's influence.

These external conditions lead to internal management conditions or structure consisting of organizational structure, employee competence, and cross-functional team involvement. The closer the chief purchasing officer is to the chief executive officer on the organizational chart, the greater the influence of the purchasing function. The higher level of purchasing employees' skills and knowledge, the greater purchasing's influence. Also, the more purchasing employees are leaders and participants in critical cross-functional teams, the more influential the function will be in strategic planning.

Each of these internal management conditions leads to overall internal influence which includes coalition building. A key contributor to coalition building is the use of metrics. In particular, metrics allow supply management to demonstrate to critical decision-makers how and where it is adding value to the business.

Each of these conditions is a prerequisite for what is termed proactive management. Proactive management adds value to the firm exploiting opportunities to manage risk. Purchasing manages risk by effectively planning and controlling outsourcing, developing long-term supplier alliances, and involving suppliers early in product planning and development.

Each of these individual conditions is necessary but not sufficient by itself for purchasing to have a high level of influence in the strategic planning process. All of the conditions must be present because they enhance each other; consequently, this is a systematic model in which each condition is dependent upon the others.

FIGURE 3
CONDITIONS THAT CREATE INFLUENCE FOR PURCHASING IN CORPORATE STRATEGIC PLANNING
(INITIAL MODEL SUBSEQUENTLY REVISED)

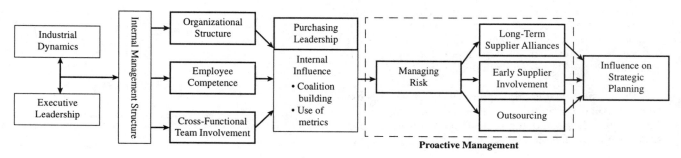

APPENDIX C: SUMMARY OF THE REVISIONS TO THE INITIAL MODEL •

When the 21 in-depth case studies of the 24 organizations were completed and the initial model developed, the model was reviewed and discussed with chief purchasing officers and their managers from four highly respected purchasing operations. Managers with a wide variety of career backgrounds and from diverse organizations were represented. In total, nine managers with more than 200 years of combined experience in 11 organizations were involved in these discussions.

The purpose of the review was to evaluate the model by gaining in-depth feedback from experienced executives who had high levels of influence in their organizations. To minimize potential bias, general overview questions were used.

But specific questions or concerns remained after the case studies. Additional information was sought about the role of purchasing leadership and the place of proactive purchasing in the model. In addition, questions remained about organizational culture in the model. Accordingly, the plan was to use probing questions if these topics emerged.

Leadership

The role of purchasing leadership quickly emerged in each of the review discussions. The discussions can be summarized by the quote from one of the vice presidents: "The CEO must open the door for purchasing, but it takes good leadership to identify, create, and take advantage of opportunities that add value to the organization."

Other pertinent statements included, "Leadership is essential so that the purchasing group is synchronized with the top executives. The CPO is the critical link." "Leadership is necessary to make sure everyone is pushing the envelope....Without effective leadership purchasing would not be able to add the necessary value.

Similar comments were heard in each of the discussions. Purchasing leadership was the overwhelming theme in the review discussions. This was consistent with the last third of the case studies so it was concluded that purchasing leadership must take a more dominant position in the model.

Proactive Purchasing Management

The second strongest theme related to the role of proactive purchasing management. Each of the discussions quickly led to the meaning of risk management to proactive management. It was easy to conclude that this was not the appropriate term for the model. After the discussions, several additional managers were asked if it would be better to simply use the term proactive management. The comments led to the decision to change the title of risk management.

More important was the role of proactive purchasing management in the model. Each of the discussions centered on this component and they directly related to purchasing leadership initiatives. After reviewing the discussion notes, three themes emerged in this order: adding value, increasing quality, and managing costs. A review of the case notes also revealed the prevalence of these themes. Accordingly, risk management was changed to proactive management with a subtitle relating to the themes mentioned earlier.

A reanalysis of the case notes and the review discussions indicated the strong relationship between purchasing leadership, and proactive management. In fact, the relationship was so strong that at one point the possibility of combining these two components in one box was considered. However, discussions with two academics and a thorough review of the cases led to the conclusion that these two themes were so strong that they both had to be separated in the model. To further emphasize the importance of these variables, they were placed at the center of the model.

Because proactive purchasing management was considered the key concept and placed in the middle of the diagram, all of the other components flowed into this concept. Accordingly, the entire diagram was reconfigured.

Three components were added to the concept of proactive purchasing: total cost management, early purchasing involvement, and total business involvement. Each of these concepts had been considered before the review discussion. During the case analysis, total cost had been considered in terms of formal models for total cost of ownership; however, it was decided that this was too restrictive. The proactive purchasing processes focused on managing total costs rather than emphasizing price. Formal models were not necessary.

Early purchasing involvement meant that purchasing did not wait to be asked to join a business activity; rather, it got involved early in the company's process initiatives or new product introductions. For instance, one organization was going through a major reorganization so that it would be structured around product groups rather than functions. Purchasing was involved in the initial stages of discussions and was intimately involved in every aspect of the process. Ultimately, purchasing became a standard member of all new product teams.

Total business involvement meant that purchasing was involved in every aspect of the business. Rather than simply responding to purchase orders from internal customers, purchasing was involved in the decision about the product quality and function. In other words, purchasing was looking for ways to add value beyond a narrow acquisition function.

Competitive Environment

From the beginning of this research, it seemed that the ratio of materials purchased to total revenues would be important. This was termed industrial dynamics but as the research progressed, this did not seem to be the correct term. A thorough review of the cases and the comments made during the review discussions further emphasized that industrial dynamics was not the correct term.

The important concept was the business's competitive environment rather than the ratio of materials purchased to total revenues. For instance, financial service firms operate in a highly competitive environment, and purchasing had a relatively high level of influence in the financial services case study. However, the ratio of goods purchased to total revenues was not high. Meanwhile, in a high technology manufacturer, the ratio of materials purchased to revenues was high but purchasing influence was low. Also, inconsistencies could be detected among the consumer products groups. What accounted for this inconsistency? It was not the industry as much as it was the competitive environment facing the executive leadership. The initial hypothesis that purchasing influence was a function of the industry was rejected. However, it was not rejected until late in the research because of the reluctance to reject an initial hypothesis that seemed logical.

Organizational Culture

Although culture varied dramatically among the case studies and had a major impact on purchasing, it could not be determined how it affected purchasing's influence. But the review discussions and follow-up questions of managers at the case sites clarified the role of culture. The main point is that purchasing's culture had to be consistent with the overall organizational culture. If the entire company had a competitive culture, purchasing had to be competitive as well. If the company had a culture that accepted change, purchasing had to be able to adjust to change as well.

In addition to consistency between the cultures, it was important that purchasing "talk the language and do business like the rest of the company." For instance, in the banking industry, it is important that purchasing professionals talk and do business like the bankers. Or in the healthcare industry, purchasing professionals must talk like the health professionals. In other words, purchasing cannot isolate itself through language. This was especially clear where people with business degrees managed the purchasing process; however, most of the other employees within the company consisted of professionals from a different professional background. Because of these observations, *congruence with organizational processes and culture* was added to the model.

Employee Competence: Business Knowledge

The final revision was the inclusion of business knowledge within the concept of employee competence. This addition resulted from a review of the case studies, the model review discussions, and numerous discussions with employers who hire new college graduates. Not only must the employees understand the purchasing process, they must fully understand the products, business, and industry in which they operate. It may be concluded that much of the purchasing process remains consistent across industries; however, purchasing is product related and operates within the context of the industry in which it is located. The healthcare context is much different than the hospitality context which is much different than high technology manufacturing. Also, each of these businesses is concerned with a much different product group. Employees must understand their companies' product group.

A common concern heard from recruiters when they are interviewing new college graduates is that new employees must learn the business quickly. Based on the cases and interviews with recruiters, it may be concluded that in the purchasing profession evaluations of employee competence are based one-third on purchasing knowledge, one-third on communication and analytical skills, and one-third on product and business knowledge.

Summary

The initial model was revised as a result of review discussions with four purchasing vice presidents and five other high level managers, reanalysis of the case notes and follow-up discussions with academics and other purchasing managers. The primary revisions included the following: (1) purchasing leadership became more dominant in the model; (2) proactive purchasing management was expanded and became the central focus of the model; (3) the term risk was eliminated; (4) the concept of industrial dynamics was changed to competitive environment; (5) congruence with organizational processes and culture was added; and (6) employee competence was expanded by adding the concept of business knowledge.

CENTER FOR ADVANCED PURCHASING STUDIES •

THE CENTER FOR ADVANCED PURCHASING STUDIES (CAPS) was established in November 1986 as the result of an affiliation agreement between the College of Business at Arizona State University and the National Association of Purchasing Management. It is located at The Arizona State University Research Park, 2055 East Centennial Circle, P.O. Box 22160, Tempe, Arizona 85285-2160 (Telephone [602] 752-2277).

The Center has three major goals to be accomplished through its research program:

1. to improve purchasing effectiveness and efficiency
2. to improve overall purchasing capability
3. to increase the competitiveness of U.S. companies in a global economy

Research published includes 27 focus studies on purchasing/materials management topics ranging from purchasing organizational relationships to CEOs' expectations of the purchasing function, as well as benchmarking reports on purchasing performance in 26 industries.

Research under way includes: *Early Supplier Involvement in New Product Design; Developing Internet Electronic Commerce Strategies for Purchasing and Supply Chain Management; Environmental Scan for Purchasing and Supply Management;* and the benchmarking reports of purchasing performance by industry.

CAPS, affiliated with two 501(c)(3) educational organizations, is funded solely by tax-deductible contributions from organizations and individuals who want to make a difference in the state of purchasing and materials management knowledge. Policy guidance is provided by the Board of Trustees consisting of: